The Political Economy of New Regionalism in Northeast Asia

This book is the first attempt to offer a holistic and integrated exploration of the political-economic framework underpinning economic regionalism. In doing so it provides a much-needed contribution to the literature on international political economy, international relations and Asian political economy in relation to economic regionalism. The existing literature provides broad generalizations and limited discussion on economic integration (i.e. free trade agreements, FTA) with most analyses of regionalism generally contained to the field of economics with a focus on the welfare implications of FTAs, both for participating countries and the world as a whole. Readers of this book can view economic regionalism from a variety of perspectives with input from Chinese, Japanese and Korean research institutes, business and industry groups and government officials. Drawing on the considerable country experience and expertise of the authors, the book attempts to unravel the paradox of the market-driven economic globalization process (regionalism) and address a serious gap in the current literature relating to the political-economic characteristics and strategies of China, Japan and Korea in relation to economic regionalism.

Chang Jae Lee is currently Visiting Senior Fellow at the Centre for International Development (CID) of the Korea Development Institute (KDI). He previously served as Vice President at the Korea Institute for International Economic Policy (KIEP). His research interests include Northeast Asian economic cooperation and East Asian economic integration.

You-il Lee is Associate Professor of International Business and Director of the King Sejong Institute Adelaide at the University of South Australia. He has published research on socio-economic and political changes caused by globalization and regionalism in Asia. He is currently working on another monograph, *The Evolution of Korean Political Economy: From Growth to Maturity* and *The Impact of Foreign Multinational Corporations in Korea*.

John Benson is Professor and Head of the School of Business at Monash University Malaysia and Adjunct Professor in the Department of Management, Monash University Australia. His most recent monographs include *Teacher Management in China: The Transformation of Educational Systems* (Routledge 2016) with Eva Huang and Ying Zhu, and *Employers' Associations in Asia: Employer Collective Action* (Routledge 2017) with Ying Zhu and Howard Gospel (editors).

Ying Zhu is Professor and Director of the Australian Centre for Asian Business at the University of South Australia. He has been working as a business leader as well as an academic leader in China and Australia for more than thirty years. He has published widely in the areas of International HRM, International Business and Economic Development in Asia.

Yoon-Jong Jang is Senior Research Fellow and Director of the Department of the Fourth Industrial Revolution at the Korea Institute for Industrial Economics and Trade (KIET). He is currently examining strategy shift in Korean industries faced with the Fourth Industrial Revolution. His publications include *Globalization and the Korean Economy* and *Socio-economic Shocks of the Fourth Industrial Revolution and Policy Responses in Korea*.

Routledge Advances in International Political Economy

Global Criminal and Sovereign Free Economies and the Demise of the Western Democracies
Dark Renaissance
Edited by Robert J. Bunker and Pamela Ligouri Bunker

Capitalist Alternatives
Models, Taxonomies, Scenarios
Paul Dragos Aligica and Vlad Tarko

International Mobility, Global Capitalism, and Changing Structures of Accumulation
Transforming the Japan-India IT Relationship
Anthony P. D'Costa

The Crisis and Renewal of American Capitalism
A Civilizational Approach to Modern American Political Economy
Edited by Laurence Cossu-Beaumont, Jacques-Henri Coste and Jean-Baptiste Velut

Globalization and Labour in the Twenty-First Century
Verity Burgmann

Emerging Market Multinationals in Europe
Edited by Louis Brennan and Caner Bakir

The Dialectics of Liquidity Crisis
An Interpretation of Explanations of the Financial Crisis of 2007–08
Chris Jefferis

The Political Economy of New Regionalism in Northeast Asia
Dynamics and Contradictions
Chang Jae Lee, You-il Lee, John Benson, Ying Zhu and Yoon-Jong Jang

For more information about this series, please visit www.routledge.com/series/IPE

The Political Economy of New Regionalism in Northeast Asia

Dynamics and Contradictions

Chang Jae Lee, You-il Lee, John Benson, Ying Zhu and Yoon-Jong Jang

Routledge
Taylor & Francis Group
LONDON AND NEW YORK

First published 2018
by Routledge
2 Park Square, Milton Park, Abingdon, Oxon OX14 4RN

and by Routledge
605 Third Avenue, New York, NY 10017

First issued in paperback 2020

Routledge is an imprint of the Taylor & Francis Group, an informa business

British Library Cataloguing-in-Publication Data
A catalogue record for this book is available from the British Library

Library of Congress Cataloging-in-Publication Data
Names: Yi, Ch'ang-jae, 1952– author.
Title: The political economy of new regionalism in Northeast Asia : dynamics and contradictions / by Chang Jae Lee [and four others].
Description: Abingdon, Oxon ; New York, NY : Routledge, 2019. | Series: Routledge advances in international political economy ; 30 | Includes bibliographical references and index.
Identifiers: LCCN 2018021963 | ISBN 9781138938984 (hardback) | ISBN 9781351051385 (ebook)
Subjects: LCSH: Regional economics—East Asia. | Regionalism—East Asia. | East Asia—Economic integration.
Classification: LCC HC460.5 .Y525 2019 | DDC 337.15—dc23
LC record available at https://lccn.loc.gov/2018021963

ISBN 13: 978-0-367-50417-5 (pbk)
ISBN 13: 978-1-138-93898-4 (hbk)

Typeset in Galliard
by Apex CoVantage, LLC

Contents

Figures

Tables

Preface

Northeast Asia, namely China, Japan and Korea (CJK), a region which accounts for about one-fifth of the world's gross domestic product, has experienced strengthened regional economic cooperation since the end of the Cold War. CJK held their first annual Trilateral Summit Meeting in 1999, on the occasion of the ASEAN (Association of Southeast Asian Nations)+3 Summit Meeting. The annual Trilateral Summit Meeting promoted tripartite cooperation in depth and scope, both at the governmental and non-governmental level. The tripartite cooperation and integration process gained further momentum when the three countries agreed to hold the first independent Trilateral Summit Meeting in 2008. Apart from the Summit Meetings, the three countries officially launched the CJK Free Trade Agreement (CJK FTA) negotiations in 2012. Following the first round of negotiations held in Seoul in 2013, there have been thirteen rounds of FTA negotiations and a number of working-level meetings have been held. The last round of negotiations was held in Seoul, South Korea between 22 and 23 March 2018. In the five years since the launch of CJK FTA negotiations, no tangible outcomes have been achieved, although some limited progress has been made. The slow progress of the CJK FTA negotiations and their limited results can be explained mainly by two factors: the lack of leadership and the weakened momentum for the CJK FTA. From the perspective of all three countries this poor performance was due to a concentration on other ongoing FTA negotiations. In addition, progress in regional economic integration has faced constant obstacles related to non-economic factors such as territorial disputes and historical issues. Due to political tensions, the Trilateral Summit Meeting was postponed for three and a half years until it resumed in November 2015. The CJK FTA negotiations are still at a preliminary stage despite the three countries managing to hold three rounds of negotiations per year. Meanwhile, the three countries have begun to experience slower economic growth, largely due to structural problems.

Within Asia, the Declaration on the ASEAN Economic Community Blueprint was adopted in November 2007. The ASEAN Economic Community (AEC) envisages: (a) a single market and production base, (b) a highly competitive economic region, (c) a region of equitable economic development and (d) a region fully integrated into the global economy. The AEC was to be established at the end of 2015, although the vision of establishing an East Asian Community was first proposed by the EAVG at the ASEAN+3 Summit in October 2001. After a decade since the EAVG submitted its report to the leaders, the East Asia Vision Group II (EAVG II) was established in October 2011 to review the ASEAN+3 cooperation over the past fifteen years and provide a future vision of the ASEAN+3 for the coming decades. The EAVG II Report was submitted to the Fifteenth ASEAN+3 Commemorative Summit in Phnom Penh on November 2012. Furthermore, the EAVG II has proposed the establishment of the East Asian Economic Community as a vision for East Asian economic integration by 2020. In this context, creating new economic growth momentum has become a top policy priority. Thus, accelerating economic integration among the three countries could serve as an important policy solution for the realization of the vision for 2020.

This book is the first attempt to offer a cohesive exploration of the political-economic framework, which comprises a detailed appraisal of the socio-economic, political and cultural changes reflected in the course of Northeast Asian regionalism. The key contributions of this attempt are to draw on the considerable country experience and expertise of the authors in attempting to unravel the paradox of the market-driven economic globalization process (regionalism) and address a serious gap in the current literature relating to the politico-economic characteristics and political-economic strategies of CJK in relation to economic regionalism.

Chang Jae Lee, You-il Lee, John Benson,
Ying Zhu, Yoon-Jong Jang
May 2018

Acknowledgements

This project was supported by the Seed Program for Korean Studies through the Ministry of Education of the Republic of Korea and the Korean Studies Promotion Service of the Academy of Korean Studies (AKS-2017-INC-2230006). We also acknowledge the initial financial support from the Small Grant Program of the Division of Business and Law at the University of South Australia.

Abbreviations

AANNZFTA	ASEAN-Australia-New Zealand Free Trade Agreement
ACP	Africa, Caribbean and Pacific
ADB	Asian Development Bank
AEC	ASEAN Economic Community
AEM	ASEAN Economic Ministers
AFTA	ASEAN Free Trade Area
AIIB	Asia Infrastructure and Investment Bank
APFTA	Asia-Pacific Fee Trade Agreement
APT	ASEAN Plus Three (China, Japan and Korea)
APTCF	ASEAN Plus Three Cooperation Fund
ASEAN	Association of South East Asian Nations
BRICS	Brazil, Russia, India, China and South Africa
CCP	Chinese Communist Party
CEPA	Closer Economic Partnership Arrangement
CEPEA	Comprehensive Economic Partnership in East Asia
CER	Closer Economic Relations
CET	Common External Tariff
CJK	China, Japan and Korea
CM	Common Market
CPTTP	Comprehensive and Progressive Agreement for Trans-Pacific Partnership
CRTA	Cross Regional Trade Agreement
CU	Customs Union
DDA	Doha Development Agenda
DJ	Former President Kim Dae-jung (Korea)
DRC	Development Research Centre of China
EAFTA	East Asia Free Trade Area
EAS	East Asia Summit
EASG	East Asia Study Group
EAVG	East Asia Vison Group
EAVG II	East Asia Vison Group II
EMU	Economic and Monetary Union
EPA	Economic Partnership Agreement

EU	European Union
FDI	Foreign Direct Investment
FTA	Free Trade Agreement
FTAAP	Free Trade Agreement of Asia Pacific
GATT	General Agreement on Tariffs and Trade
GCC	Gulf Cooperation Council
GDP	Gross Domestic Product
HMT	Hong Kong, Macao and Taiwan
HT	Hong Kong and Taiwan
ICT	Information and Communication Technology
IIA	International Investment Agreement
IMF	International Monetary Fund
JETRO	Japanese External Trade Organization
JSC	Joint Study Committee
KIEP	Korea Institute for International Economic Policy
KIET	Korea Institute for Industrial Economics and Trade
KORUS	Korea and United States
KOTRA	Korea Trade and Investment Promotion Agency
MAFF	Ministry of Agriculture, Forestry and Fisheries (Japan)
METI	Ministry of Economy, Trade and Industry (Japan)
MNC	Multinational Corporation
NAFTA	North American Free Trade Agreement
NEAC	North-East Asian Conference on Environmental Cooperation
NEASPEC	North-East Asia Sub Regional Program on Environmental Cooperation
NET	Natural Economic Territory
NIRA	National Institute for Research Advancement (Japan)
PTA	Preferential Trade Agreement/Arrangement
RCEP	Regional Comprehensive Economic Partnership
R/O	Request and Offer
ROO	Rules of Origin
RTA	Regional Trade Agreement
SPS	Sanitary and Phytosanitary Measures
TBT	Technical Barriers to Trade
TCS	Trilateral Cooperation Secretariat
THAAD	Terminal High Altitude Area Defence
TNC	Trade Negotiating Committee
TPP	Trans-Pacific Partnership
TRADP	Tumen River Area Development Program
TRIPS	Trade-Related Aspects of Intellectual Property Rights
TSS	Trilateral Summit Meeting
UNCTAD	United Nations Conference on Trade and Development
UNDP	United Nations Development Program
US	United States of America
WTO	World Trade Organization

1 New regionalism in Northeast Asia[1]

Introduction

Until the emergence of the People's Republic of China (hereafter China) as a global economic powerhouse in the late twentieth/early twenty-first century, the global economic clustering or regional integration worldwide had been led and dominated by Europe (European Union) and the United States of America (US). Since the launch of the World Trade Organization (WTO) in 1995, free trade agreements (FTAs)[2] have increased rapidly. This is partly because of the shift of both the US and the EU's perception of economic regionalism, which refers in general to regional and institutional arrangements to encourage and facilitate the free flow of goods and services between countries in the concerned geographic region.[3] Previously, the US and the European Union (EU) considered traditional regionalism as 'a stumbling block' which discouraged the expansion of free trade.[4] However, since the inauguration of the North American Free Trade Agreement (NAFTA) in 1994 and EU in 1992, these regions have changed their stance and now consider FTAs as 'a building block' which can work in synergy with multilateralism and free trade[5] (Krueger 1999).[6]

Modes of integration/regionalism

Traditional modes of economic integration (old regionalism), based largely on the theory of comparative advantage (mostly found in the theory of customs union), can be represented by the static effects of economic integration (shallow economic integration); a term coined and developed by Viner (1950) and Lipsey (1957 and 1960).[7] According to Lawrence (1997), this mode of shallow integration is government-led and is associated with import-substitution and trade mostly in industrial products. In this model, geographical closeness is "a key ingredient for the establishment of preferential trade relations in that lower transportation and transaction costs foster trade concentration, and the greater likelihood of sharing cultural, economic, linguistic or political ties facilitate the tasks of policy coordination" (Solis and Katada 2007: 60). On the other hand, due to the rapid process of economic globalization,[8] a new form of economic integration emerged in the late 1990s. This new form, emphasizing economic efficiency, arose out of the dynamics effects of increased competition, foreign direct investment and the effects of economies of scale, technology transfer and improved productivity (Burfisher, Robinson and Thierfelder 2004).[9]

One of the most striking features of today's global political-economic geography is the shift in countries' traditional policy orientation based on market-driven multilateralism (Burfisher, Robinson and Thierfelder 2004; Baier, Bergstrand and Egger 2006). Among the most noticeable features of this new form of economic integration/global development (or new regionalism) is the increased depth of integration and cooperation (regional trade agreement (RTA)/free trade agreement), particularly in East Asia since the early 1990s (Solis and Katada 2007). The development was pioneered by the Association of Southeast Asian Nations (ASEAN) in 1992 when it initiated the ASEAN free trade area (AFTA) (Munakata 2002) and RCEP (regional comprehensive economic partnership), which is a trade bloc between ASEAN, three of the Northeast Asian economies (i.e. China, Japan and South Korea, hereafter Korea) and Australia, India and New Zealand (Solis and Katada 2007). In Krueger's own words,

> Although the concrete actions necessary to bring about a true free trade area either in the western hemisphere or across the Pacific remain to be agreed upon, it is clear that the emphasis of the world trading regime has shifted from one in which trade relations between nations were almost entirely multilateral to one in which the open multilateral system coexists with a series of preferential arrangements.
>
> (Krueger 1999: 109)

Pempel's (2005b) work has also recognized this new phenomenon. Pempel writes that "regional integration in East Asia has been historically slow to develop cross-border linkages and regional connections through much of the later nineteenth and twentieth centuries" and

> despite such a fragmented historical legacy, East Asia has, with varying degrees of depth and speed, and with admittedly numerous reverses over time, begun to put into place an expanding network of webs that span national borders and deepen regional ties.
>
> (Pempel 2005a: 5–6)

Consistent with Lawrence's (1997) definition of the new regionalism, the current process of deeper economic integration shows the following contrasting characteristics compared with the old regionalism: (a) export-orientation; (b) foreign direct investment led by private firms; and (c) trade including all goods, services and capital-intensive products (Lawrence 1997: 19). Katada (2009a: 1) defines this market-based economic cooperation as "regionalization" or "regional concentration of economic flows" (Mansfield and Milner 1999: 591), which is a "bottom-up approach of the regional integration led by private sector business activities and subnational communication through people's activities such as migration". In this bottom-up process or functionalist approach, the integration is a function of actors cooperating across state borders to better achieve key tasks. Baldwin's work on twenty-first-century regionalism (2011) provides useful distinctions of the new form of regionalism:

> In a nutshell, 21st century regionalism is not primarily about preferential market access as was the case for 20th century regionalism; it is about disciplines that underpin the trade investment-service nexus. This means that 21st century regionalism is driven by a different set of political economy forces; the basic bargain is "foreign factories for domestic reforms" – not "exchange of market access". As 21st century regionalism is largely about regulation rather than tariffs, regulatory economics is needed rather than Vinerian tax economics. Finally, 21st century regionalism is a serious threat to the WTO's centrality in global trade governance, but not for the reason suggested by the old building-stumbling-block thinking. 21st century regionalism is a threat to the WTO's role as a rule writer, not as a tariff cutter.
>
> (Baldwin 2011: 3)

Among the most noticeable features of the new global development is the stepping up of economic regionalism efforts towards integration and cooperation (regional trade agreement/free trade agreement) particularly in Asia. As of June 2017, 659 notifications of Regional Trade Agreement (RTAs) had been received by the WTO and its predecessor the General Agreement on Tariffs and Trade (GATT). These WTO figures correspond to 445 physical RTAs of which 279 are currently in force. Over 20 per cent of the 279 agreements in force were FTAs (free trade agreements) wherein one of the signatories was an East Asian country (WTO 2017). With a growing interest in institutional economic integration, East Asia overshadowed Northeast Asia and has become the main context of regional economic integration. The focus of Northeast Asian economic cooperation gradually shifted from sub-regional functional economic integration, encompassing all Northeast countries and regions, to institutional economic integration among the three major Northeast Asian countries (i.e. China, Japan and Korea, herein referred to as CJK) that are involved in institutional/functional economic integration in East Asia.

By 2011, ninety-three free trade agreements involving Asian countries were in effect, up from twenty-five in 2000 (Kastner 2011). RTAs or FTAs in Asian regionalism have spread like "wildfire" (Baldwin and Carpenter 2009). Baldwin and Carpenter (2009) extend their theory of the 'building block' or 'domino theory of regionalism' to the case of the newly emerged East Asian regionalism and referred to it as the "Asian version of domino theory of regionalism". They suggested the new trend can be explained by three distinctive phases of regionalism (Baldwin and Carpenter 2009: 5–7):

- First phase – mid 1980s to 1990: during this phase, regional tariff cutting was driving nations' desire to attract the manufacturing jobs being offered by private firms (mostly from Japan, Korea, Hong Kong, Singapore and Taiwan) while they were setting up 'Factory Asia';

- Second phase – 1990s to 2000: this phase saw intra-regional trade expand rapidly as the gradual opening of China accelerated the development of Factory Asia; and
- Third phase – 2000 to present: this phase was initiated by China's suggestion in November 2000, that it might be willing to negotiate a FTA with the RCEP (ASEAN+6) (i.e. CJK + Australia, New Zealand and India).

It is noteworthy that the strong push towards economic clustering in Northeast Asia strengthened considerably after the 1997 Asian financial crisis. With a growing interest in institutional economic integration, East Asia overshadowing Northeast Asia has become the main context of regional economic integration. The focus of Northeast Asian economic cooperation gradually shifted from sub-regional functional economic integration encompassing all Northeast countries and regions to institutional economic integration among the three major Northeast Asian countries (China, Japan and Korea, or CJK) that are involved in institutional/functional economic integration in East Asia. This new move towards economic integration among states in Northeast Asia is striking given that Northeast Asia (particularly CJK) has been the most inactive in terms of economic integration due to the long-standing hegemonic competition between China and Japan, strong ties with the US, lack of institutional leadership in the region, historical animosity (Japan's Pacific War with China and its annexation of Korea between 1910 and 1945) and ongoing territorial disputes between CJK, all of which have been viewed as major obstacles in realizing successful economic regionalism in the region.

The launch of the CJK FTA negotiations was announced at the CJK Economic and Trade Ministers' Meeting held in Phnom Penh, Cambodia, on 20 November 2012. Negotiations between the three countries took over a decade to reach this stage. The most fundamental and obvious rationale behind this decision is that despite some Sino-Japanese rivalry, differences in political systems, current territorial and historical disputes and a lack of community consciousness, there have been some real economic benefits from the deepening of regional economic interdependence in recent years. These include geographic and psychic (cultural) proximity, complementary endowments of production factors and increasing economic ties. During 2012, China was the largest trading partner of Korea and Japan, and the two countries were regarded as China's second largest trading partners. In 2012, Japan was Korea's second largest trading partner and Korea was Japan's third largest trading partner (Korean Ministry of Foreign Affairs and Trade 2013).

The emergence of a new regional economic architecture in Northeast Asia raises important political-economic questions about the implications of the present global political-economic structures. While it is not possible to assess comprehensively the diverse, complex and sensitive issues primarily related to the historical, cultural, political and economic characteristics of the region, this book analyses the economic-centred approach to regionalism and demonstrates the need for a more comprehensive political-economic approach to economic regionalism (Mansfield and Milner 1999). In examining the new regionalism in Northeast Asia, this book incorporates a variety of theoretical elements, for example, international political economy, international factor mobility, the role of imperfect competition and rent seeking behaviour. Moreover, political-economic considerations such as potential conflicts between regionalism and multilateralism, and "complex patterns of capital movement and the importance of state policies and domestic market growth as contributing factors" (MacIntyre 1990: 148–149) need also to be recognized (Burfisher, Robinson and Thierfelder 2004). Northeast Asian economic cooperation has only been sporadically achieved, and its future remains uncertain primarily due to the historical, cultural, political, international and economic characteristics of the region and the strong resistance from interest groups in each nation. Nevertheless, we argue that important economic benefits are derived from regionalism, as well as strong political and economic pressures and expectations that motivate the economies of Northeast Asia to work towards integration. The active engagement towards Northeast Asian regionalism is a major response to the rapidly changing internal and external political-economic environment rather than a simple calculation based on economic optimality. As such, this move towards regional integration presents a wide range of economic and political challenges and opportunities for neighbouring countries.

Key questions and propositions

Further development of CJK integration is possible, but it is premature to expect that China, Japan and Korea's political and economic systems are soon to be homogenized. This will certainly require joint political commitment from the governments of all three countries and the political leadership to realize the regional integration is the key development to ensure economic prosperity and political stability. As for the way forward, the emergence of this Northeast Asian community and the nascent political and economic cooperation among CJK will require a strategic repositioning of other economic partners in the Asia-Pacific region, such as the US and Australia, given they have a strong economic interest in this region. The future trend of regional economic integration could develop along two competing parallel trajectories: one is an initial China-led CJK economic cluster, expanding to the CJK+ASEAN Free Trade Area, and at a later stage a further expansion to form the ASEAN+6 Free Trade Area which will cover a large part of the Asia-Pacific region, including Australia, New Zealand and India. However, this development and formation of regional integration will exclude the participation of the US. It is unclear under the Trump administration whether this is a concern for the US. If it is, then it leads to a second possible trajectory where the US forms a competing regional economic group by promoting and strengthening the formation of the Asian Free Trade Agreement, which includes the major partners of the US but excludes China.

An equally important consideration is the view held by many academics, members of the business community and policy makers who doubt the feasibility of this new regional economic architecture in Northeast Asia. Although the integration appears to be purely economic and functional (regionalization, meaning regional integration led by private sector business activities and subnational communication through people's activities), it has shown considerable progress in the market sector. Trade arrangements are influenced to a greater extent by political factors than by economic factors. Such cases of regional integration as the EU and NAFTA demonstrate that political security plays a crucial role in establishing regional integration. Therefore, the economic case for Northeast Asian regional integration is likely to be accompanied by a range of political or non-economic factors. The regional institution-building or economic integration between CJK is in its very early stages and there remains considerable uncertainty around such a FTA.

Another aspect to be noted is China's aggressive move towards regional FTA formation and its increasing interest in realizing a CJK FTA. Such an agreement would give China a foothold for further integration in Asia, free up production supply chains (concentration on manufacturing), offer enhanced economic security for the Chinese leadership, enable China to expand the use of Renminbi so that the country could internationalize its currency and reduce its reliance on the US dollar, see a greater volume of higher quality products exported to China and offer improved market opportunities for both state-owned enterprises (SOEs) and private companies. Therefore, the following questions and propositions to explore the repositioning of political and economic relationships among CJK will be examined in this book:

1 What is the current state of play and how advanced are the plans for regional integration between CJK? Can the integration continue to work in the future?
2 Who will benefit most among CJK from this new form of economic integration? What are the political and economic gains?
3 How will the uncertain prospects for stability in Northeast Asia due to historical and cultural animosities, and differences in political, social and historical perspectives, influence the shape and level of the economic integration?
4 How will changes of leadership in CJK influence the progress of CJK FTA negotiations that began in early 2013?
5 What are the critical issues and challenges for the realization of the CJK economic clustering, especially as viewed by CJK?

These questions give rise to seven key propositions which will inform the research and underpin the arguments presented in the book:

Proposition 1: Despite the significant implications of economic and political arrangements in Northeast Asia and the pressure for change and advancement, much of the literature on economic integration (i.e. FTAs) seems to be within the field of economics focusing on the welfare implications of FTAs, both for members and the world (Choi 2013).

Proposition 2: CJK's active progress on regionalism is a response to the rapidly changing political economy of Northeast Asia rather than a simple calculation based on economic optimality.

Proposition 3: While Northeast Asian economic cooperation has only been sporadically achieved and its future remains uncertain, there are not only economic benefits from the realization of the CJK FTA but also strong political and economic pressures and expectations that motivate each nation to push for the CJK FTA.

Proposition 4: Resumption of the CJK FTA talks in recent years is a response to the rapidly changing internal and external political-economic environment rather than a simple calculation based on economic optimality. As such, this move towards regionalism presents a wide range of economic and political challenges and opportunities for neighbouring countries.

Proposition 5: The TPP (Trans-Pacific Partnership) and RCEP (Regional Comprehensive Economic Partnership) (FTAAP – Free Trade Agreement of Asia-Pacific) may lead to a new form of geo-political power game between the US, China and Japan, which inevitably carries political and security implications.[10]

Proposition 6: Each country will be trying to shape economic cooperation groupings in Southeast and Northeast Asia and in the wider Asia-Pacific region to promote its respective economic interests. This may have unpredictable, unproductive and even dangerous political consequences for the CJK FTA or Northeast Asian economic integration in the near future.

Proposition 7: China's progressive approach to the new Asian regionalism (i.e. AIIB – Asian Infrastructure Investment Bank, RCEP and FTAAP) reduces the influence of the US's preferred Asian regional architecture (i.e. the TPP). The TPP (or similar arrangements) will be a major challenge to China's ambition to achieve a Peaceful Rise.

Methodology

This study is a combination of strong pre-existing and working knowledge of the political economies of three countries (China, Japan and Korea) with fieldwork which was performed in all three countries throughout 2012 and 2013. Due to the exploratory, theory-building nature of this research, interviews with key informants, combined with critical published and unpublished secondary data (e.g. industry statistics and government data) are the most appropriate methodology. The success of the project critically depends on the discussions with Chinese, Japanese and Korean research institutes, business groups, industry and government officials. As such, in-depth interviews were used as the primary method for data collection. This method has been widely used in studies of international business management because it satisfactorily meets the criteria of qualitative research: informational adequacy and efficiency as set out by Zelditch (1962).

Interviews were conducted in 2012 and 2013. This included over thirty face-to-face interviews with government officials, scholars and industry personnel who were closely associated with the CJK FTA proposal. The most compelling evidence gathered from our interviews conducted in CJK was that all parties recognized and understood the economic inter-dependency between CJK. During April 2012, we visited Korea (Seoul) for interviews with the Australian Embassy in Korea, Korean Ministry of Foreign Affairs and Trade, KOTRA (Korea Trade and Investment Promotion Agency), Korea Institute of International Economic Policy (KIEP) and Korea Institute for Industrial Economics and Trade (KIET). In September 2013 we revisited the institutions in Korea. In October 2013, we visited and conducted interviews with scholars and policy makers in Japan (Tokyo) and China (Beijing) including the Australian Embassy in Tokyo, Tokyo Denki University, Meiji University, Tsukuba University (Tokyo), the National Institute for Research Advancement (NIRA) in Tokyo and Chinese Academy of Social Sciences in Beijing. This research is, in part, based on findings from the above field works carried out in the region. This research is the first original study conducted which critically examines the evolution of the political economy of Northeast Asian regionalism based on in-depth interviews and primary data from CJK.

Given the highly sensitive nature of the data collected, confidentiality was guaranteed, and the names of interviewees are not given in the book. A list of questions for in-depth interviews and unstructured open-ended format was developed based on the research framework and the findings from the pilot interviews. Interviews were taped, transcribed and subsequently interrogated, then deconstructed. In this way, according to the principles of grounded theory, findings and theories naturally emerged from the data rather than being forced by prior hypotheses (Glaser and Strauss 1967; Bailey 1987). However, it should be said that one of the weaknesses of this approach is that the sample was relatively small and the responses were therefore indicative of general perceptions, rather than conclusive.

Structure of the book

This book consists of seven chapters including the introductory chapter. After a brief outline of the emergence of new attempts at economic integration and regionalism in Northeast Asia, Chapter 2 provides a conceptual and theoretical discussion on integration and regionalism ranging from the traditional economic approach to international political-economic insights. This chapter allows the subsequent chapters and discussion to be located within these contemporary developments and theoretical perspectives.

Chapter 3 focuses on the economic evolution relating to the emergence of the new regionalism in Northeast Asia and the main debate over geopolitics in Northeast Asia. The chapter examines the early years and transformation of Northeast Asia economic cooperation before examining the economic status and relationships between CJK countries. The analysis of the size of these economies

(GDP, trade and FDI) as well as the bilateral trade and investment flows are particularly important in this chapter, which provides a context for the institutional discussions that occur in the next chapter and later in the book.

As alluded to above, Chapter 4 explores recent attempts at institutional building between China, Japan and Korea. This process began after the Asian financial crisis and was focused on bringing together countries of East Asia. The CJK FTA negotiations are placed in this context and the chapter outlines the framework for institutional building including top level summit meetings, ministerial meetings and joint research. The chapter considers the joint studies underpinning a CJK FTA and assesses the progress to date towards a CJK FTA. The chapter concludes by suggesting that the CJK FTA is a necessary condition for the achievement of the era of East Asia.

Chapter 5 explores the current state of play of CJK using data collected from interviews and primary sources. The chapter primarily focuses on the current position as seen by various players in the three participant countries. This highlights the views of the key stakeholders and their various positions from their own country perspective, as well as the complexity of the process. This diversity and complexity illustrates the formable task facing each country in attempting to realize such a FTA and the kind of opposition that can be expected. Political issues and implications such as leadership, territorial disputes and regional stability, including a rebalancing of the geo-political situation are also considered.

Chapter 6 discusses the current debate over the political and economic rationale for the newly emerged regional architecture in Northeast Asia. It examines the rationale for the East Asia economic integration followed by assessment of the institutional integration. Issues such as relationships with various other FTAs (e.g. RECEP), possible expansion linking with the ASEAN FTA (i.e. ASEAN + CJK FTA) and Asian trade bloc (i.e. CJK + ASEAN/RCEP) are also addressed. The chapter considers countervailing forces and developments, and the limitations of economic integration.

The conclusion provided in Chapter 7 crystallizes and evaluates the significance of the findings of this study. The evolution of the political economy of Northeast Asian regionalism has been rapid with significant developments occurring since the late 1990s. This pace of change means that the dynamics and inherent contradictions need to be appraised. Throughout the book, qualitative insights will thus be provided into how specific historical, international political-economic, cultural and institutional relations form and shape the configuration of economic integration and political and economic policies, and their influences on regionalism.

Conclusion

The book has three major strengths. First, it provides a cohesive exploration of the political-economic framework, which comprises a detailed appraisal of the socio-economic, political and cultural changes reflected in the course of Northeast Asian regionalism. Second, the book draws on the considerable country experience and expertise of the authors in attempting to unravel the paradox of the market-driven economic globalization process (regionalism). Third, this book addresses a serious gap in the current literature relating to the political-economic characteristics and political-economic strategies of CJK in relation to economic regionalism.

Notes

1 Though the precise area of Northeast Asia varies, it normally includes China, Japan, the Korean peninsula (South and North Korea), Mongolia and the eastern part of Russia. In terms of economic strength, China, Japan and South Korea comprise the core of the region. References to South Korea mean the Republic of Korea unless otherwise noted. As such, throughout this paper, Northeast Asia refers to China, Japan and Korea. East Asia in this study includes Northeast and Southeast Asia but excludes the United States, Latin America, Australia, New Zealand and the Pacific Islands (Solis and Katada 2007: 229), T.J. Pempel has provided a comprehensive discussion on East Asia as a region and we follow his definition of 'region' as "contiguous territorial areas having sufficiently clear internal cohesion and definitive enough external boundaries as to be readily distinguishable from other neighboring, and purportedly equally easy-to-distinguish, regions of the world" (Pempel 2005b: 4).

2 Free trade agreement (FTA) can be defined as an economic/trade agreement between two countries or regional groupings on tariffs, duties and other trade barriers that the concerned countries impose on imports and exports. There are three different types of trade agreement, namely unilateral, bilateral and multilateral trade agreement. The unilateral trade agreement takes place when a country imposes trade barriers and restrictions and no other member or country reciprocates; whereas a bilateral agreement occurs when two countries agree to eliminate trade restrictions. The multilateral trade agreement takes place when three or regional groupings agree to eliminate tariffs and other trade barriers. FTAs can form part of a regional trade agreement (RTA), which is a reciprocal trade agreement between two or more countries. There are five different types of RTAs, namely, preferential trade agreement (PTA), FTA, customs union, common market and economic union. Different types of RTAs are detailed in Chapter 2.

3 In terms of a political-economic definition of 'regionalism', we adopt Fishlow and Haggard's definition of regionalism as 'a political process characterized by economic policy cooperation and coordination among countries' (Mansfield and Milner 1999: 591).

4 In his comparative analysis between multilateral (building block) and bilateral trade agreements (stumbling block), Philip I. Levy (1997), expressed a view shared by other economists in arguing that the bilateral free trade agreement undermines political support for further multilateral trade liberalization. According to Levy, "If a bilateral trade agreement offers disproportionately large gains to key agents in a country, it can never increase political support for multilateral free trade" (Levy 1997: 506).

5 With regard to 'building blocks', Richard Baldwin (1995) argues that regionalism fosters multilateral trade liberalization by raising the incentives of outside countries to join the existing trading bloc (i.e. domino effect) and it (Free Trade Agreement, bilateral trading bloc) will lead the regionalism to the path to economic globalization (free trade).

6 Krueger (1999) summarizes both arguments supporting a positive effect of regionalism on multilateralism ('building blocks'), as well as a negative effect ('stumbling blocks'). See also Baldwin (2006).

7 Robert Lipsey, a pioneer in the study of economic integration, defines the customs union as a 'branch of tariff theory which deals with the effect of geographically discriminatory changes in trade barriers' (Lipsey 1960: 496).
8 We use Shangquan Gao's definition of economic globalization as the "increasing interdependence of world economies as a result of the growing scale of cross-border trade of commodities and services, flow of international capital and wide and rapid spread of technologies. It reflects the continuing expansion and mutual integration of market frontiers and is an irreversible trend for the economic development in the whole world at the turn of the millennium. The rapid growing significance of information in all types of productive activities and marketization are the two major driving forces for economic globalization" (Gao 2000: 1).
9 More of the conceptual and theoretical discussion on the economic integration can be found in Chapter 2.
10 A detailed discussion on various types of economic blocs (i.e. TPP and RCEP) can be found in Chapters 2 and 3 in this study.

2 Regionalism in Northeast Asia

A new paradigm?

Introduction

This chapter locates the development of CJK within the rapidly changing patterns of economic integration in the global economy. A variety of theoretical paradigms are surveyed, ranging from traditional economic approaches to political-economic explanations, within which the dynamics of deeper economic integration may be viewed.

Economic integration

Over the past thirty years, functional economic integration has progressed rapidly among the three major Northeast Asian countries (CJK). The share of intra-regional trade between China, Japan and Korea increased from 12.3 per cent in 1990 to 24.1 per cent in 2014. When Hong Kong, Macao and Taiwan (HMT) are included, the share of intra-regional trade of Northeast Asia (CJK+HMT) amounted to 34.8 per cent in 2015. In addition, efforts to institutionalize Northeast Asian economic cooperation have also been made by the three countries.

Political-led regional integration

At the ASEAN (Association of Southeast Asian Nations, 10 members)[1]+3 (CJK) Summit Meeting, which was held in Manila in November 1999, the leaders of China, Japan and Korea met for a historic gathering, and since then the Trilateral Summit Meeting has taken place annually. Subsequently, the first independent Trilateral Summit Meeting took place in Fukuoka in December 2008, outside the ASEAN+3 framework. This meeting has become an annual event. Furthermore, although the three Northeast Asian countries were latecomers to economic regionalism, they have concluded a significant number of FTAs. They have not, however, managed to conclude a FTA among themselves, although some progress has been made since the commencement of the 1997 Asian financial crisis.[2]

Based on a recommendation proposed by the Trilateral Joint Study Committee, which was set up following the agreement among three leaders at the Manila Summit in 1999, the leaders agreed to launch an Official Tripartite Joint Study for a CJK FTA at the Trilateral Summit Meeting in Beijing in October 2009. Seven meetings of the Joint Study Committee for a CJK FTA were held between May 2010 and December 2011. The outcome of this Joint Study Committee was submitted to the leaders at the Trilateral Summit Meeting (TSM) in 2012.

There were six TSMs held between 2011 and 2015 until the outbreak of territorial conflicts between Korea and Japan, and North Korea's nuclear provocation. On the other hand, another interesting development regarding regionalism is the number of bilateral and plurilateral FTAs that have been concluded among East Asian countries since the turn of this century. ASEAN concluded FTAs with China, Korea and Japan respectively.

With the proliferation of FTAs among the East Asian countries, the interest in a region-wide FTA in East Asia has increased. The idea of an EAFTA (East Asia Free Trade Area) was first recommended by the East Asia Vision Group in October 2001 and was also proposed as a mid and long-term goal by the East Asia Study Group in November 2002. This was followed by an EAFTA Study by experts from ASEAN+3 countries, CEPEA (Comprehensive Economic Partnership in East Asia) and ASEAN+6 (CJK + Australia, New Zealand and India). Based on their recommendations, four government-level working groups were established to prepare a region-wide FTA in East Asia, the area being by this time a major part of global manufacturing. This grouping later became known as the Regional Comprehensive Economic Partnership (RCEP, ASEAN+6 FTA negotiations) and was formally launched in November 2012 at the ASEAN Summit in Cambodia.

East Asia's policy makers are increasingly of the view that a CJK FTA could provide a strong foundation for a possible EAFTA, ASEAN RCEP and eventually a Japanese-led CEPEA, involving Australia, New Zealand and India. This new centre of Northeast Asian economic power will undoubtedly rival that of the North America FTA and the US-led Trans Pacific Partnership (TPP).[3] Both these FTAs involving the US are now, however, under some scrutiny by the Trump administration. Notwithstanding, the proposed CJK FTA would most likely have a similar impact on Europe, namely decreased trade and investment with the three member countries. Currently, the EU has a FTA with Korea, but not with China or Japan. In addition, with the exception of Norway, none of the European countries is in FTA talks with China. Switzerland is the only European country with a FTA with Japan. Equally significant, CJK did not have a bilateral FTA with Australia until December 2014.[4] While the economic reality of increased interdependence surfaced later for Europe, in the case of CJK, the intensity of economic interaction was the basis for considering greater integration (Yap 2005).

Increased economic interaction since the Asian financial crisis has led to increased interest in institutional integration in the Asian region. Following the first ASEAN+3 Summit Meeting which was held in Kuala Lumpur in December 1997, the Summit Meetings as well as Ministerial and Senior Officials Meetings have taken place regularly. Such meetings constitute a strong framework for regional economic cooperation among the ASEAN+3 countries. Additionally, the East Asia Summit Meeting was launched in 2005. Functional economic integration has also been advancing in East Asia. Over the past twenty years, the share of intra-regional trade among ASEAN+3 countries rose from 28.6 per cent to 39.7 per cent. In 2010, the share of intra-regional trade among ASEAN+3+HMT, ASEAN+6 and ASEAN+6+HMT represented 51.9 per cent, 45.1 per cent and 56.2 per cent respectively, surpassing that of the North American Free Trade Agreement (NAFTA) (40.5 per cent) and nearing the level of the EU (56.3 per cent). This increase in regional trade has led to a number of bilateral and plurilateral FTAs being concluded among East Asian countries since the turn of the century. In particular, and of relevance to this book, ASEAN has concluded FTAs with China, Korea and Japan.

Global political-led integration

Running parallel to the above-mentioned events, the Doha round of trade talks commenced in November 2001. These negotiations, also known as the Doha Development Round or Doha Development Agenda (DDA), were designed to free up trade in agriculture, services and manufactured goods, and represented the latest attempt at multilateral trade negotiations between every member of the WTO. Its goal was to complete negotiations by January 2005, although that deadline was subsequently postponed to 2006. The talks were finally suspended in June 2006 followed by the WTO official declaration of the end of the talks in December 2015. The major stumbling block was that the US, the EU and emerging developing counties failed to reach an agreement to reduce agricultural subsidies.

The failure of the DDA reflects three significant changes in the global economic system. First, a larger systemic shift in the global economy with the emergence of BRICS (Brazil, Russia, India, China and South Africa) has led to a paradigm shift within the system of the WTO (or the US and the EU) led multilateral trade talks. Second, the new millennium saw the rapid growth of bilateral RTAs with free trade areas, which has demonstrated to WTO members that bilateral RTAs can be a viable alternative to a global economic system.[5] Third, many Asian countries (i.e. ASEAN) began to use FTA formation as a strategy to enhance their bargaining position in multilateral trade negotiations within the WTO; in particular, regional integration became a high priority in national policy making. As such, the pursuit of FTAs is one of the important strategies to strengthen bargaining position in negotiations (Kim 2008: 61). Given that the economic prospects for the US and the EU are presently rather gloomy, East Asia is expected by many to be the engine of world economic growth and we may yet witness the start of the East Asia era in the twenty-first century.

In order to realize the era of East Asia, the region will need to maintain its economic growth, enlarge internal markets and create a stable international political and security environment. To satisfy these conditions, a region-wide FTA in East Asia is needed. Given the many FTAs formed among East Asian countries, including ASEAN+1 FTAs, the remaining missing link is the link among the three major Northeast Asian countries. The fundamental task to accomplish a region-wide FTA in East Asia is thus the formation of a FTA or FTAs between China, Japan and Korea. As such, the vision of realizing the East Asia era could be used as an additional stimulus to push forward the formation of a CJK FTA.

As stated above, with the stalled WTO negotiations, the increasingly rapid process of economic globalization, the changing structure of the international political economy from bipolar to unipolar, and the wide but rapid spread of regional economic integration in Asia, the future of multilateral liberalization (traditional form of economic integration) has become bleak (Kim 2008: 60). In contrast, regional trade agreements (RTAs), including bilateral agreements on free trade areas, continue to multiply making a new form of regionalism the most active mode of trade liberalization in this millennium as evidenced in East Asia (i.e. RCEP-ASEAN with Northeast Asia). The regionalization of trade is a serious concern to many international economists who view multilateralism as far superior to regionalism for improving global welfare. The key issue is the preferential nature of regional agreements, which could divert trade and reduce the potential for future multilateral liberalization (Baldwin and Freund 2011: 121).

New regionalism: conceptual insights

The search for factors and motives affecting foreign investment behaviour became fashionable in the 1960s and 1970s when foreign investment emerged as an important economic issue in the global political economy. Up until the late 1970s, most theoretical works on international trade, the international division of labour and intra-industry trade relied on the concept of comparative advantage introduced and developed within key elements of Ricardian trade theory with Swedish economists Heckscher and Ohlin's framework (Davis 1995: 201–226). The essence of the Heckscher-Ohlin model is that the commodity composition of trade between nation-states is determined mainly in accordance with the pattern of factor endowments (e.g. capital, labour, land and natural resources) of the trading countries and the production process of the commodities traded based on perfect competition. This shows a sharp contrast with the earlier Ricardian model (1817) which emphasizes differences in technology, labour time cost and labour productivity between countries as the cause of patterns of international trade (Kiljunen 1989: 110).

The Heckscher-Ohlin economic approach to international trade rests on several key assumptions. These include constant returns to scale, a common worldwide stock of technological knowledge, identical tastes and preferences among countries and no country-specific resources or factors of production. Based on these assumptions, it follows that a country will find a comparative advantage in goods which use its relatively abundant factors of production relatively intensively. In other words, relatively labour-abundant (developing) countries are predicted by the theory to have a comparative advantage in relatively labour-intensive goods, while relatively capital-intensive (developed) countries find a comparative advantage in capital-intensive goods (Riedel 1991: 112–114). This approach is based on the belief that the most efficient allocation of resources in response to the supply and demand of goods and services and rapid economic growth (or development) should be achieved by the functioning of the free market mechanism. When combined with an analysis of the role of the international division of labour and the investment of capital as an engine of growth, this leads to the further conclusion of the desirability of freedom from state intervention in international trade and economic activity.

Classical economic theorists regard foreign direct investment as a capital flow "which increases the stock of capital in the host country" (Moran and Katsikeas 1997). At a time when shortage of capital was regarded as a major obstacle to development in the Third World, direct foreign investment seemed to offer an attractive way of breaking out of the vicious circle of poverty" (Jenkins 1987: 18). Graham and Krugman (1979) further argue that foreign direct investment (FDI) should be regarded as a facilitating device for international trade in goods, services and intangible assets, such as knowledge. Behavioural economic approaches can also be extracted from various works. These include, for example, Hymer's (1976) industrial organization (IO) theory, Buckley and Casson's (1976) internalization theory, Vernon's (1966) and Well's (1968) product cycle theory and Dunning's (1995) eclectic theory. The essential and common assertion of these approaches is that a firm's decision to relocate its production sites overseas is a direct response to market-imperfection (Hymer 1976: 24–27).

A theory that has been designed to fill the missing gap between the IO and product cycle theory, and the theory of internalization is Dunning's (1988b: 13–70) 'eclectic paradigm' of international production. This is a convergence between the theory of the determinants of comparative advantage in international trade and the theory of the determinants of international production. While Dunning (1988a) sees internalization as key to understanding the behaviour of MNCs, he also considers the fundamental question of why a firm might want to produce abroad at all.

The principle hypothesis of the eclectic theory of international production is that the internationalization of capital takes place in four systematic stages in the relationship between the country's position in the development cycle and its investment pattern. In the first stage, when a country is poor, there is little inward or outward investment. As the country begins the development process, it enters the second stage when there is an increasing inflow of FDI. In the third stage of development, the country experiences increasing outward investment and decreasing inward investment and then in the final stage, it emerges as a net exporter of capital and a capital investor.

The essence of the Dunning's eclectic approach is made up of three distinctive or necessary conditions for the internationalization of capital. An investing firm must possess competitive or ownership advantages (e.g. property rights, production management, organizational and marketing skills and innovatory capacity), vis-à-vis its competitors to outweigh the disadvantage of being foreign. These ownership advantages take the form of the possession of intangible assets, which are, at least for a period of time, specific to the firm possessing them. Such advantages include proprietary technology, patented trademarks, superior managerial knowledge and marketing techniques. Foreign investment takes place when the benefits of internalizing the ownership advantages are useful and beneficial to the investing firm and when they are greater than any other means of profit-maximization. Assuming the above two conditions are satisfied, it must be in the global interests of the enterprise to utilize these advantages in conjunction with at least some factor inputs outside its home country. This is determined by location-specific advantages which include abundance of high-quality, lower labour cost, cheap raw materials and more favourable investment environments and policy-determined costs arising from trade restrictions, low transportation cost, labour legislation and pollution controls (Dunning 1988b: 26–27).

In the absence of any of these three conditions a firm will tend to serve the foreign market through exports. Similarly, the greater the degree to which the three conditions are met, the more likely the firm is to engage in the possession of ownership-specific advantages as a necessary pre-requisite for involvement in FDI. This paradigm shows a strong intention to synthesize the major elements of the aforementioned theories of foreign investment. In doing so it provides a framework for a comparison between dominant paradigms, to establish common ground and to clarify the relationship between the various levels of analyses and questions which economists have been concerned about addressing.

Conventional trade theory has been criticized by other international economy theorists. The neo-classical view opposes the theory of free trade based on perfect competition and argues that international trade is largely driven by economies of scale rather than comparative advantage or simply capital contribution in which this view also holds that international markets are generally imperfectly competitive (Krugman 1987: 131–144; Riedel 1991: 113–114). In other words, complete specialization, imperfect competition and differences across economies in technologies and consumer preferences can reverse the model of dynamics of international trade (factor production) developed by Heckscher and Ohlin (Baldwin 2008). The nascent theories of foreign direct investment based on the above assumption that the MNCs, which are the product of imperfect competition, provide an added challenge to the Heckscher-Ohlin approach (Dunning 1988a: 2–3). Thus, among economists, there emerges a strong necessity that trade theory (classical) and the theory of foreign direct investment (neo-classical) should be integrated (Hofmann 2013; Moran and Katsikeas 1997).

Integration of trade (government-led) and FDI (individual firm-led) can be viewed as part of a new form of economic regionalism, where collective decision-making is central to facilitating regional arrangements (Katada 2009a) and "the design and implementation of a set of preferential policies within a regional grouping of countries aimed at the encouragement of the exchange of goods and/or factors between members of the group" (Wyatt 1995: 78). We use the conceptual framework of one of the earlier functionalists, Lindberg (1963), in which 'integration' is defined as "the development of devices and processes for arriving at collective decisions by means other than autonomous action by national governments" (Cited in Laursen 2008: 4). As Wolf (2002: 7) argued, "Governments of member states are locked in to the integration process and they have little room to manoeuvre. The structural and functional implications of trans-border exchanges inevitably coerce national governments into greater degrees of cooperation, coordination and integration". Economic integration can begin with a simple preferential trade area agreement (e.g. the development of free trade and factor mobility). As integration increases between states, agreements develop towards a common market and eventual complete economic and monetary union such as is happening in various stages, with the European Union, the North American Free Trade Agreement (NAFTA) and the Andean Community and Mercosur (trading blocs of South America).

A FTA is a different level of trade agreement towards economic integration, which generally takes place in stages where tariffs are progressively lowered and ultimately barriers to trade are removed among member states. The lowest level of integration is known as Preferential Trade Agreement or Preferential Trade Arrangement (PTA), which is a trading bloc and allows member states (at least two or more) to grant the other participants preferential access to select segments of their markets. This is normally done by reducing tariffs but not by abolishing them completely. An example of a PTA can be found in bilateral agreements between ASEAN and China, and the EU and the ACP (African, Caribbean and Pacific) countries and more recently mega-PTAs such as the RCEP and the TPP. Although the line between a PTA and a free trade area (FTA) is not always clear, a PTA can still be regarded as the first level of economic integration since most PTAs have a main goal of becoming a FTA (Panagariya 2000).

The next level of integration is a Free Trade Area. A FTA is a PTA in which member countries do not impose any trade barriers (zero tariffs) on goods produced within the union. A group of countries who have jointly signed a free trade agreement (FT) eliminate pre-existing tariffs, import quotas and preferences on most of goods and services among signatory members. However, each country keeps its own tariff barriers (tariffs and import quotas) to trade with non-members. In an effort to avoid tariff evasion (through re-exportation), the countries in a FTA are required to use a system of certification of origin most commonly called 'rules of origin' that require a member country to provide evidence of the minimum levels of local material inputs and local transformations adding value to the goods. This would allow goods that meet these minimum requirements to gain preferential treatment envisioned by the free trade area provisions (WTO 2017). A key objective of this integration is to achieve free market principles (specialization and international division of labour) that would allow the member countries to reduce tariffs and ensure the free flow of goods and services (non-government intervention) through their comparative advantage. An important reminder for this level of economic integration is that members of the FTA do not have to be in the same or geographical proximity. The EU has signed a FTA with Korea and some African nations such as South Africa and Tunisia.

The next level of economic integration is known as a customs union (CU). A CU is an intergovernmental agreement based on free market principles, especially reduction of trade barriers. As such, this type of agreement resembles the early stages of integration and is a type of trade bloc. With the CU, trade barriers are not only eliminated but a common external tariff established vis-à-vis third parties. A common market typically adds more criteria to a CU such as implementing similar product regulations and permitting the free flow of factors of production between member countries. CUs do not have the same rules of origin systems as a free trade area; any product entered into the CU would be subject to the same tariff. Some countries choose a CU over a FTA for political reasons (deeper integration), such as a pre-requisite for the future establishment of a political union (Andriamananjara 2011: 112). In short, members entering into a free trade agreement (FTA) remove tariff barriers between members, and together and collectively apply a common (unified) external tariff (CET) against non-members.

The effect of a CU can be explained by Viner's (1950) international trade theory of 'trade creation and trade diversion' (Balassa 1967). In line with Ricardo's (1817) comparative advantage theory, trade creation allows more efficient members to sell larger volumes to less efficient (domestic) members, whereas more efficient non-members may sell fewer goods to members, creating greater opportunities for less efficient members to capitalize by selling more – a concept known as trade diversion (Economics Online). Lipsey defines the CU as a "branch of tariff theory which deals with the effect of geographically discriminatory changes in trade barriers" (Lipsey 1960: 496). A CU may arise from different sources such as (a) the specialization of production according to comparative advantage which is the basis of the classical case for the gains from trade, (b) economies of scale, (c) changes in the terms of trade, (d) forced changes in efficiency due to increased foreign competition and (f) a change in the rate of economic growth (Lipsey 1960: 469).

According to the theory of custom unions, if the gains from trade creation outweigh the losses from trade diversion, then membership of a customs union will increase the welfare of member countries. However, the theory behind comparative advantage does not seem to predict the bilateral trade relationships. Helpman and Krugman (1985) who developed and theorized the gravity model of international (bilateral) trade, fills the missing gap in predicting multilateral and bilateral trade flows. The theory's analytical basis is the economic size (often using Gross Domestic Product (GDP) measurements – GDP and the product of GDP) and psychic distance between two countries. In addition to these variables, the model uses other explanatory variables, including distance, population size and GDP per capita, land areas and geographical and cultural proximity such as "common borders, common languages and common membership in regional trading agreements" (Frankel 1997: 50), to predict the possibility and desirability of FTA formation and facilitation of 'natural' trading blocs.

The fourth level of economic integration is known as a common market (CM). The CM is also known as a "factor integration" (Jovanovic 2006: 120–169) as the agreement between governments is to allow members free access and unrestricted movement of goods and services, as well as labour and real and intellectual capital. CMs are often regarded as the first stage of establishing a single market, which requires governments to collaborate in additional policy areas to ensure comparable treatment in all countries. As in the earlier stages of economic integration, the goal of CM is to gain economic efficiency through free markets. In principle, with unfettered mobility, labour and capital can respond to economic signals within the common market with greater ease, resulting in a more efficient allocation of resources and the "utilization of all potential opportunities of efficient division of labour" (Hosny 2013: 133). As shown in Table 2.1, most of the regional trade agreements that Asian countries have established (e.g. ASEAN with Korea, Australia and China) can be considered as a prior stage to the CM.

The most advanced type of economic integration is the economic union, where the monetary and fiscal policies of member states are harmonized and sometimes completely unified. This is usually referred to as 'policy integration'. One

Table 2.1 Custom unions in force and planned

Agreement	*Date*
	In force
Southern African Customs Union (SACU)	1910
Switzerland-Liechtenstein	1924
European Union (EU)	1 January 1958
Central American Common Market (CACM)	12 October 1961
Caribbean Community (CARICOM)	1 August 1973
Andean Community (CAN)	25 May 1988
EU-Andorra	1 July 1991
Southern Cone Common Market (Mercosur, Mercado Común del Sur)	29 November 1991
Israel-Palestinian Authority	1994
EU-Turkey	1 January 1996
Eurasian Economic Community (EAEC)	8 October 1997
Economic and Monetary Community of Central Africa (CEMAC, Communauté Économique et Monétaire de l'Afrique Centrale)	24 June 1999
West African Economic and Monetary Union/Union Économique et Monétaire Ouest-Africaine (WAEMU/UEMOA)	1 January 2000
East African Community (EAC)	7 July 2000
EU-San Marino	1 April 2002
Gulf Cooperation Council (GCC)	1 January 2003
Customs Union of Belarus, Kazakhstan and Russia	1 July 2010
	Planned
Arab Customs Union (ACU)	2015
Southern African Development Community (SADC)	2010
Economic Community of Central African States (ECCAS)	2011
Economic Community of West African States (ECOWAS)	2015
African Economic Community (AEC)	2019
Arab Common Market (ACM)	2020
Australia-New Zealand Closer Economic Relations Trade Agreement (ANZCERTA)	2020

Source: Andriamananjara 2011: 112.

extreme case of an economic union is a monetary union (MU). A good example of the former is the European Union with its single currency, the Euro. When an economic union involves a unifying currency, it can become the next stage of economic integration, which is called an economic and monetary union (EMU). An EMU with a single economic market, a common trade policy, a single currency, a common monetary policy, together with a single fiscal policy, including common tax and benefit rates, represents complete harmonization of all policies, rates and economic trade rules.

The above observation of the different stages of open regionalism or economic globalization has tended to be the predominant contemporary form of the new regionalism. Burfisher, Robinson and Thierfelder (2004: 10–11) sum up the key characteristics of the new regionalism that may involve many of the elements found in the deepest level of integration and which can be found, to varying degrees, in the recent process of economic regionalism in Europe and Asia. These characteristics include:

- facilitating financial and FDI flows
- liberalizing movement of labour within the agreed member countries
- harmonizing domestic tax and subsidy policies
- harmonizing macro policies, including fiscal and monetary policy, including coordinated exchange rate policy among member countries
- establishing institutions to manage and facilitate integration (e.g. regional development funds, institutions to set standards and dispute resolution mechanisms)
- improving communications and transportation infrastructures to facilitate increased trade and factor mobility
- harmonizing legal regulation of product and factor markets (e.g. anti-trust law, commercial law, labour relations and financial institutions)
- completing the establishment of a single market with a common currency and an integrated monetary and exchange rate policy.

A critique of traditional regional integration theory can also be found in the Marxist perspective by writers like Henderson (1986), Holloway (1994), Jenkins (1987), Kiely (1994) and MacIntyre (1990). The common theme in this literature is that social relations such as the role of the state, international political economy, geographical, historical and cultural standards in relation to internationalization of capital and the process of economic integration is largely overstated in both the traditional and the neo-classical theories of international trade and capital flows. In his study of American MNCs in the 1980s, MacIntyre (1990) shows how the state can retain influence over international capital flows and FDI behaviour should be viewed within the process of the restructuring of capitalist social relations. He further suggests that although the cost factor did characterize much of FDI behaviour of the US MNCs, particularly in sun-set industries, "complex patterns of capital movement and the importance of state policies and domestic market growth as contributing factors"

(MacIntyre 1990: 148–149) should also be recognized. The logic underpinning this view is that international capital flows are based on "institutional and political conditions and market demand in the host country, and cultural, political and economic ties between host and home" (MacIntyre 1990: 150).

To some extent the case of economic globalization (new regionalism), the exchange of goods and products, and international capital flows are based on "institutional and political conditions and market demand, and cultural, political and economic ties between host and home" (MacIntyre 1990: 150). This is contrary to the basis of economic integration theory (traditional and new regionalism), which focuses heavily on free market principles (e.g. specialization, international division of labour, comparative advantage, factor endowment and efficiency in resource allocation). According to free market-oriented theories on regionalism/economic integration, as economic integration increases, the barriers of trade between markets diminish.

Balassa (1967) believed that supranational common markets, with their free movement of economic factors across national borders, naturally generate demand for further integration. This is not only economic (through monetary unions) but also political and thus, economic communities naturally evolve into 'political unions' over time. In other words, the neo-liberal approaches seem to ignore the complexities in the process of economic integration and that these complexities are significantly guided by many other variables beyond the factor endowments or comparative advantages. This market-driven economic model which emphasizes the potential economic benefits is narrowly conceived.

In the case of political integration, it can be the process "whereby nations forgo the desire and ability to conduct foreign and key domestic policies independently of each other, seeking instead to make joint decisions or to delegate the decision-making process to new central organs" (Lindberg 1963: 6). Put simply, economic and political cooperation are necessary for integration to continue to deepen (a new form of regionalism). As integration goes beyond trade, it will result in the formation of regional institutions, increased interaction between both states and societies and a mutual desire for security. This does not mean that there have not been any market-based regional cooperative efforts or rationalization among the members of Northeast Asia. As will be seen in the rest of this book, the new phenomenon of economic integration in Northeast Asia since the late 1990s suggests that an assessment of structural and institutional changes, such as socio-political and economic changes during capitalist industrialization in the region, is required. Additionally, other different forms of structural adjustments in the course of economic development will need to be explored.

An insight into the relationship between members' comparative advantage and its economic integration within relative factor endowments is a useful starting point in assessing the main drivers of economic integration in the earlier years of regionalism in Europe. However, the macro-economic approach (comparative advantage) seems to ignore the fact that the process of industrial relocation differs significantly according to conditions in both the home and host countries. FDI is in many cases guided by many other variables beyond the comparative advantage factor. As will be seen in the rest of this book, the new phenomenon of regionalism in Asia since the late 1990s suggests an assessment of structural and institutional changes, such as socio-political and economic changes during capitalist industrialization, which offers a richer analysis of deeper regional integration. These variables should include the changing nature of national economic interests, and the industrial policies among the trade blocs in response to the changing environment of the domestic and international political economy.

Conclusion

In analysing the new regionalism in Northeast Asia, this book incorporates a variety of theoretical elements. The international political economy, international factor mobility, the role of imperfect competition, rent-seeking behaviour and political-economy considerations such as potential conflicts between regionalism and multilateralism, capital flows, state policies and domestic market growth are some of the elements that should be recognized (Burfisher, Robinson and Thierfelder 2004; MacIntyre 1990).

We argue that while Northeast Asian economic cooperation has only been sporadically achieved and its future remains uncertain, primarily due to the historical, cultural, political, international and economic characteristics of the region and the strong resistance from interest groups in each nation, not only are there economic benefits from regionalism but there are also strong political and economic pressures and expectations that motivate the economies of the Northeast Asia to push for integration. The active engagement towards Northeast Asian regionalism is a response to the rapidly changing internal and external political economy environment rather than a simple calculation based on economic optimality. This move towards regionalism presents a wide range of economic and political challenges and opportunities for neighbouring countries.

Notes

1 ASEAN consists of ten countries, including Indonesia, Malaysia, the Philippines, Singapore and Thailand who formed the association in 1967, Brunei (joined in 1984), Vietnam (1995), Laos and Myanmar (1997) and Cambodia (1999).

2 In 1997 a major financial crisis affected much of Asia and impacted on the world economy. The last quarter of 1997 was the worst financial performance in the history of post-war Asian economies and cast some doubt on the so-called 'Asian Miracle'. In addition to the major currency problems among Association of Southeast Asian Nations (ASEAN), including Indonesia, Thailand, the Philippines and Malaysia, Hong Kong's stock market fell 10.4 per cent in October and 14 per cent in January 1998, which was the biggest percentage fall in the Hang Seng in more than five years. In the year to January 1998, the Indonesian currency rupiah fell 258 per cent against the American dollar, the Thai baht, 107 per cent, the Philippine peso 69 per cent, and the Malaysian ringgit 83 per cent respectively. These problems spread to more developed economies. Japan's fourth largest broker, Yamaichi, declared bankruptcy on 24 November 1997 and subsequently the seventh largest broker Sanyo Securities, declared bankruptcy on 3 December 1997. These events provoked considerable concern among foreign investors and the wider

global economy. The rapid exodus of foreign and local investors and the drying up of internal and external financial resources due to the foreign exchange losses following the sharp depreciation of Asian currencies clearly reflected the degree of foreign concern.

3 The US returned to Asia with a new free trade concept, 'competitive liberalization', (Bergsten 1996a and Bergsten 1996b) followed by 'pivot or rebalance' to Asia policy redirecting the US foreign policy from the Middle East and Europe to Asia in the form of Trans Pacific Partnership (TPP), which was former US president Obama's signature trade deals and appears to challenge the underpinnings of the CJK FTA. The TPP also known as the Pacific Four (P4) agreement, is a plurilateral FTA between Brunei Darussalam, Chile, New Zealand and Singapore that came into force in May 2006. In fact, it is the political implications of being part of this 'higher level' of integration (high politics) that has the potential to affect the political-economic geography of Northeast Asia. The recent (January 2017) issue of a letter submitted by the Office of the US Trade Representative (USTR) to signatories of the TPP agreement stating that the US had formally withdrawn from the agreement as per guidance from the President of the US (Office of the United States Trade Representative 2017), led to a new turning point for the architecture of the East Asian political economy. With the advent of the Trump administration the term, 'pivot' or 'rebalance' has officially disappeared in accordance with the US official withdrawal from the TPP. This Asia policy has been replaced with a new strategy, 'America First' (Panda 2017).

4 The emergence of this Northeast Asian community and the nascent political and economic cooperation between CJK will require a strategic repositioning of other economic partners in the Asia-Pacific region, particularly Australia, given that the nation has a strong economic interest in this region. Recent trade statistics that show the significance of Australia's trade with Northeast Asia (China, Japan and Korea), demonstrates the importance of those countries to Australia's economic well-being. In 2014 Australia's trade volume (export/import) with these countries (AUD$ 257.3 billion) far exceeded the combined total (AUD$ 171.7 billion) of trade with the United States (US) and the European Union (EU) (DFAT 2015). In 2014 this region accounted for 39.7 per cent of Australia's two-way trade worldwide (DFAT 2015). In particular, China has become Australia's largest two-way trading partner; Japan was its second largest partner for two-way trade and Korea was ranked its fourth largest trading partner followed by the United States. In fact, undoubtedly one of the most fundamental and obvious reasons behind Australia's strong and sustained economic performance in recent years (Australia has grown 10 per cent since the start of the global financial crisis up to 2011 and has the lowest unemployment rate (5.2 per cent) among the OECD member countries) is its strong trade and economic links with the emerging economies of Asia, the powerhouse of global economic growth. As such the potential success of the Northeast Asian economic integration is a potentially significant issue for Australia as the future of Australia is increasingly dependent on Asia. That future will be determined substantially by the ability of the Australian economy to compete in a variety of business arenas in this region. The relationship between CJK and Australia will be discussed in Chapter 5 of this book.

5 For further and extensive discussion on DDA, see Keating (2015).

3 The evolution of Northeast Asian economic cooperation

Introduction

This chapter begins with a discussion on the evolution of Northeast Asian regionalism, addressing the reason for the emergence of this form of economic clustering in Northeast Asia. We then examine how the economic status of the three CJK countries has changed and how functional economic integration has proceeded among them in terms of trade and investment.

Early years of Northeast Asian economic cooperation

Following the end of the Cold War in the late 1980s, the debate on Northeast Asian economic cooperation began within academic circles. Subsequently, Korea's establishment of diplomatic relations with the Soviet Union in 1990 and with China in 1992 helped set up a favourable environment for Northeast Asian economic cooperation by removing major obstacles to regional cooperation. At the time Northeast Asian countries differed quite significantly in terms of their comparative economic competitiveness.

China and, to a lesser degree, North Korea, possessed a pool of cheap but quality labour and were rich in natural resources, while the Soviet Union had plentiful untapped natural resources and a solid base in basic sciences. Mongolia also possessed various natural resources. Japan boasted abundant capital and advanced technologies, whereas Korea (South) had recent development know-how and production technology. Given these complementary endowments of production factors among Northeast Asian countries, Northeast Asian economic cooperation appeared to have great promise. This potential led to high expectations for Northeast Asian economic cooperation. There existed, however, many serious obstacles to this economic cooperation such as diverse political and economic systems, lingering historical and political issues, disparate levels of economic development and a lack of infrastructure in the region. These factors were expected to limit and shape the nature of Northeast Asian economic cooperation.

Under these circumstances, no serious attempt was made to see Northeast Asian economic cooperation as being a case of formal economic integration similar to the EU or NAFTA. Instead, economic cooperation between proximate localities across national boundaries has been regarded as the most probable type of Northeast Asian economic cooperation, and it has mainly been viewed as consisting of diverse ways of enhancing ongoing functional economic integration. Cooperation has included trade, investment, human and cultural exchanges among the neighbouring localities and addressing cross-border infrastructure issues such as transportation and railroad construction, as well as natural resource development projects. Numerous conferences have been held in different parts of the region to discuss ways to promote trade and other types of economic cooperation between localities in the East Sea (Sea of Japan) rim, Yellow Sea rim and the Gulf of Bohai areas.

As a result, several ideas were proposed: Scalapino's (1998) Natural Economic Territory (NET) provided a basic concept with which to understand Northeast Asian economic cooperation as embodying local economic integration. Scalapino (1998) recognized the trend of increasing interaction between NET economies; that is, "economic entities that cross political boundaries, taking advantage of the complementarity of neighboring regions, combining resources, manpower, capital, technology and managerial skills. With political barriers being progressively lowered, this trend is certain to be expanded in the years ahead" (Scalapino 1998: 1). His 1998 analysis is still valid today:

> Bilateralism will continue to dominate interstate relations due to the diversity of the states of this region, but multilateralism will gradually expand, with a concert of states the most logical route. Institutionalized multilateral institutions exclusively Northeast Asian, face many obstacles, with the initial ones likely to be in the economic realm. The growth of NETs, however, is already taking place, and is destined to play a major role in bringing the region into greater economic integration.
>
> (Scalapino 1998: 22)

Sohn's (1995) Linear Free Trade Area Model[1] was also an attempt to conceptualize Northeast Asian economic cooperation. Those who see Northeast Asian economic cooperation mainly as sub-regional integration naturally adopted quite a strict definition of Northeast Asia's geographical boundaries to encompass North and South Korea, Japan, China's north eastern provinces (Liaoning, Jilin and Heilongjiang),[2] the Russian Far East and Mongolia. The merits and limitations of a strict geographic definition of Northeast Asia lie in the fact that it includes only a part of China. Since China has a huge territory, it has an advantage in highlighting NET-type economic cooperation. However, its critical limitation is the exclusion of other parts of China, which makes it more difficult for China's central government to participate in the discussion of Northeast Asian economic cooperation.

The alternative approach to Northeast Asian economic cooperation thus starts from a broad geographical definition of Northeast Asia: South and North Korea, Japan, all of China, Hong Kong, Taiwan, Mongolia and the Russian Far East and Siberia. For the advocates of this approach, Northeast Asian economic cooperation cannot be interpreted as merely local integration. First, a broad geographical definition expands the region to encompass an area larger than the EU. Second, the assertion is that there are many ways to pursue economic cooperation in Northeast Asia, not all of which can be classified as local economic integration. Besides economic ties between neighbouring localities, diverse types of cooperation such as infrastructure development in telecommunications and transportation, energy development, fisheries cooperation, science and technology cooperation, environmental cooperation and other factors can be included in the context of Northeast Asian economic cooperation.[3] This approach differs from the above-mentioned in that it regards Northeast Asian economic cooperation as a comprehensive economic cooperation, even though conditions may not be ready for institutional economic integration.

Initially, it was environment cooperation that assisted the building process of the institutional framework for Northeast Asian economic cooperation. In the early 1990s various meetings, such as the North-East Asia Sub-regional Program on Environmental Cooperation (NEASPEC), the North-East Asian Conference on Environmental Cooperation (NEAC) and the China-Japan-Korea Environment Ministers' Meeting, were held. In addition, the Tumen River Area Development Program (TRADP) deserves special mention. This project, aimed at pursuing Northeast Asian Economic Cooperation by developing border areas of China, Russia and North Korea, had merit as a multilateral attempt to develop a specific, geo-politically sensitive area, under the leadership of an international organization. Moreover, since it was pursued along with North Korea's Rajin-Sunbong Free Trade Zone, the project was expected to alleviate political tension in Northeast Asia. The idea of developing the Tumen area into a golden triangle was proposed at the Conference on Northeast Asian Economic and Technical Cooperation, held in Jilin Province, China, in 1990. Subsequently, TRADP was launched by the United Nations Development Program (UNDP) as a regional cooperation program in 1991. In 1995, the initial five-member countries (People's Republic of China, Democratic People's Republic of Korea, Mongolia, Republic of Korea and Russian Federation) signed agreements for the establishment of the intergovernmental mechanism, namely, the TRADP Consultative Commission, at the Vice-Minister level. In 1998, the Tumen Secretariat was founded in Beijing under the UNDP.[4]

Despite huge expectations for Northeast Asian economic cooperation in the early years, no substantial progress was made for a number of reasons. First, although the local governments tried to establish joint projects to enhance Northeast Asian economic cooperation, it was very difficult for them to realize any project of significance without the help of central governments. Especially in the case of China and Russia (Soviet Union), it was mainly the provincial governments that had keen interest in Northeast Asian economic cooperation, while their central governments were not significantly active. Given this mismatch of central and provincial governments, it was difficult to advance Northeast Asian economic cooperation.

Second, North Korea could not pursue any meaningful open-door policy or economic reform, and thus became a serious stumbling block. Additionally, amid its nation building and economic reform, Russia could not pay serious attention to Northeast Asian economic cooperation. Third, non-economic barriers among Northeast Asian countries stemming from their historical legacies were difficult to overcome. Fourth, the lack of infrastructure in key areas such as transportation and energy, and the limited legal framework for economic cooperation, combined to become a hindrance to the realization of joint economic projects. Considering that many important economic cooperation projects focused on natural resource development and infrastructure building, it was difficult to make any significant progress for Northeast Asian economic cooperation without overcoming at least some of these obstacles.

Transformation of Northeast Asian economic cooperation

While Northeast Asian economic cooperation was encountering various difficulties, two new important developments significantly changed the nature of and the potential for Northeast Asian economic cooperation. First, regionalism became a worldwide phenomenon in the 1990s. Regionalism originated in Europe in the 1950s, and as the United States abandoned its long-standing opposition to regionalism in the late 1980s, many developing and transition economies adopted it in the 1990s. Among the Northeast Asian countries, the three major Northeast Asian countries – China, Japan and Korea – joined the FTA (free trade agreement) movement belatedly at the turn of the century, although they have pursued several bilateral and plurilateral FTAs within a relatively short period of time.

Second, the Asian financial crisis of 1997–1998 prompted many East Asians to consider the need for institutionalizing regional economic cooperation.[5] The first Summit Meeting, as discussed earlier, was held among the leaders of the ASEAN+3 (China, Japan and Korea) countries in Kuala Lumpur in December 1997, and evolved into the ASEAN+3 framework consisting of regularly held Summit Meetings and Ministerial Meetings for discussion on economic cooperation among thirteen East Asian countries. Thus, with a growing interest in institutional economic integration, East Asia overshadowing Northeast Asia has become the main context of regional economic integration. Moreover, the focus of Northeast Asian economic cooperation gradually shifted from subregional functional economic integration, encompassing all Northeast countries and regions, to institutional economic integration among the three major Northeast Asian countries that are involved in institutional economic integration in East Asia.

Economic status of China, Japan and Korea

Gross domestic product (GDP)

The economic status of China, Japan and Korea in the world has grown markedly over the past twenty-five years. The global share of GDP of the three economies increased from 16.2 per cent in 1990 to 22.5 per cent in 2015.[6] Their share rose to 21.5 per cent in 1995 before dropping to 17.0 per cent in 1998 with the effect of the Asian financial crisis. It then rebounded to 19.5 per cent in 2000 before diminishing continuously to 15.6 per cent in 2007, and in the wake of the global financial crisis, it reached the highest level in 2015 (see Figure 3.1). However, the trends varied quite significantly from one country to another. During the same period, China's share soared enormously from 1.7 per cent to 15.0 per cent. Propped up by a long-lasting rapid economic growth, China's share continued to rise from 1995 until 2015. In marked contrast, Japan's share shrank substantially from 13.3 per cent in 1990 to 5.6 per cent in 2015. After a short growth phase in the early 1990s when its share reached 17.5 per cent in 1994, Japan showed a declining tendency for the next two decades. During the same period, Korea's share increased from 1.2 per cent to 1.9 per cent. The country's share rose to 1.9 per cent in 1996 before dropping to 1.2 per cent in 1998 due to the Asian financial crisis. Korea's share bounced back to 2.0 per cent in 2006 before declining to 1.5 per cent in 2009 in the aftermath of the global financial crisis, rebounding since then to 1.9 per cent in 2015.

In considering these three countries, it is interesting to note the reversal in size between the Chinese and Japanese economies over the past twenty-five years. As shown in Figure 3.2, China caught up with Japan in terms of economic size in 2009. The size of the Chinese GDP, which amounted to a mere 13 per cent of the Japanese GDP in 1990, grew to 50 per cent of that recorded in 2005, and became slightly larger in 2009. In 2014 and 2015, Chinese GDP was 227 per cent and 266 per cent respectively of the Japanese GDP (see Figure 3.2).

Korea's GDP, which represented 70.4 per cent and 9.0 per cent of that of China and Japan respectively in 1990, accounted for 12.5 per cent and 33.4 per cent of China's and Japan's GDP respectively, in 2015.

Trade

Over the past twenty-five years, the status of China, Japan and Korea in terms of trade volumes showed a similar trend. The share of the three countries in the world's total exports increased continuously from 11.9 per cent in 1990 to 20.8 per cent in 2015[7] with only a few exceptions (see Figure 3.3).[8] During the same period, the share of China's exports soared from 1.8 per cent to 13.8 per cent, and that of Japanese exports diminished from 8.2 per cent to 3.8 per cent, while Korea's share expanded from 1.9 per cent to 3.2 per cent.

For the period 1990 to 2015, the share of CJK in the world's imports rose almost continuously from 10.0 per cent to 16.5 per cent[9] with only a few exceptions (see Figure 3.4).[10] The share of China's imports rose from 1.5 per cent to 10.0 per cent, and that of Japan's imports shrank from 6.5 per cent to 3.9 per cent, while Korea's share increased from 1.9 per cent to 2.6 per cent. As in the case of GDP, a reversal of trade volumes between China and Japan also occurred, although the reversal of trade volumes happened earlier than that of GDP: China caught up with Japan in terms of export and import volumes in 2004 and in

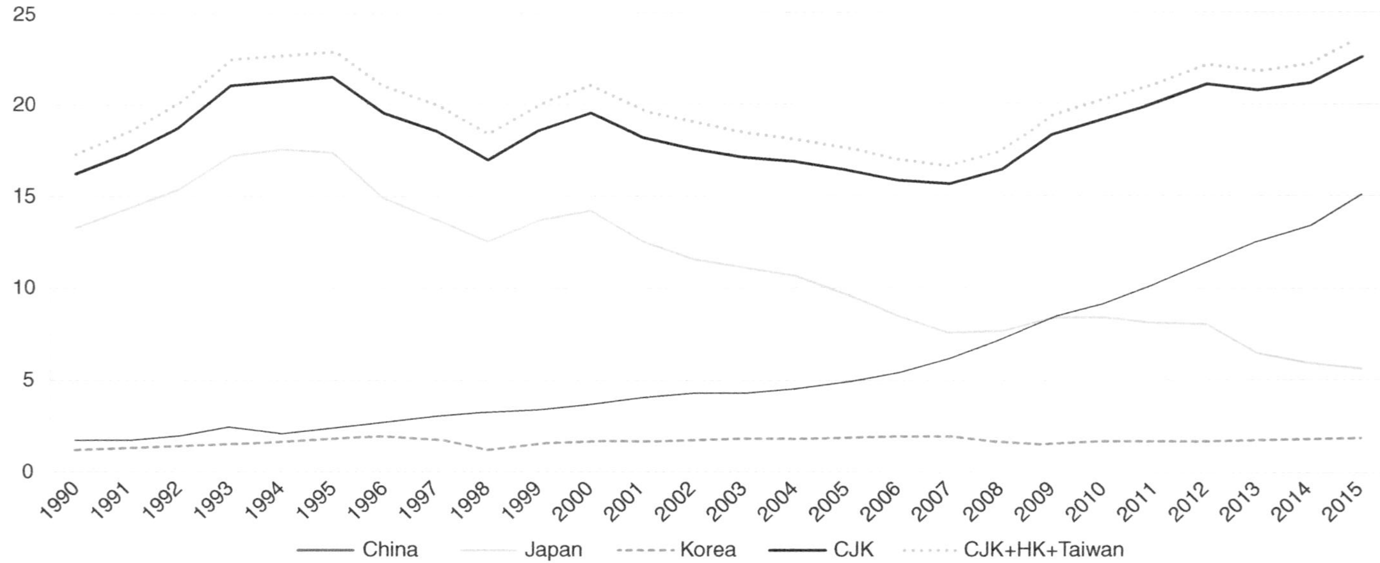

Figure 3.1 Share of China, Japan and Korea in the world's total GDP (%)

Source: IMF, World Economic Outlook 2016 (accessed on 3 June 2016).

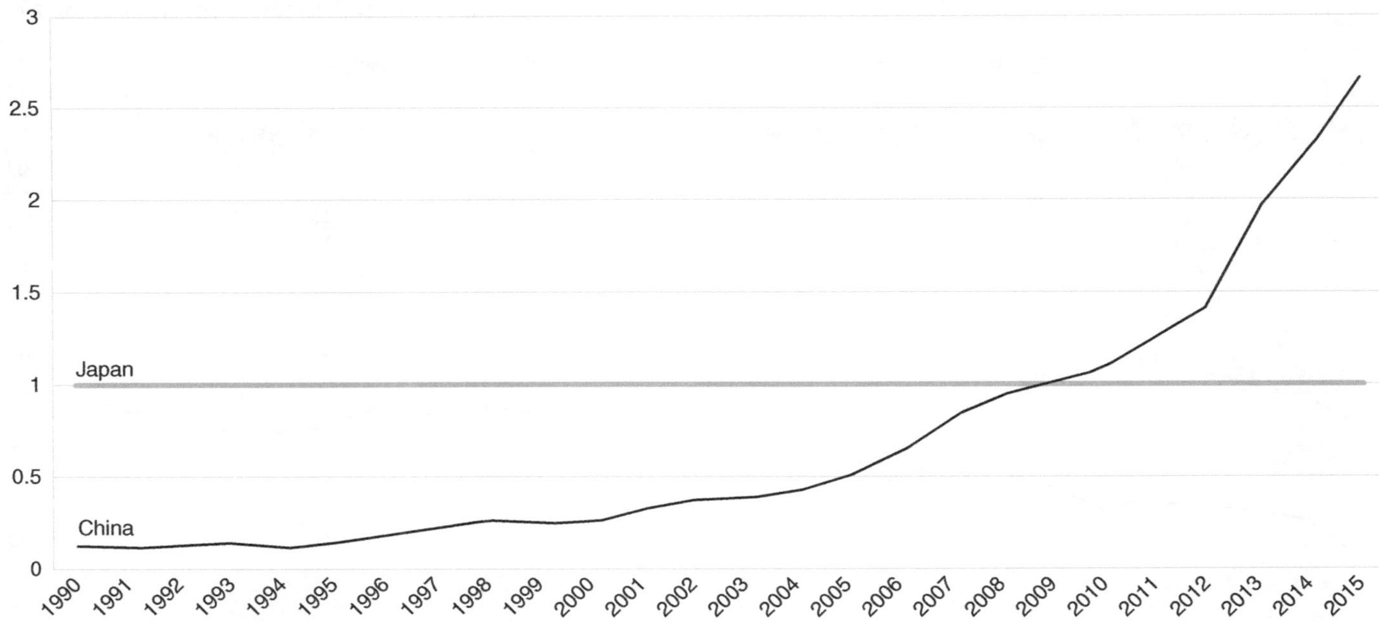

Figure 3.2 China's GDP compared to that of Japan

Source: IMF, World Economic Outlook 2016 (accessed on 3 June 2016).

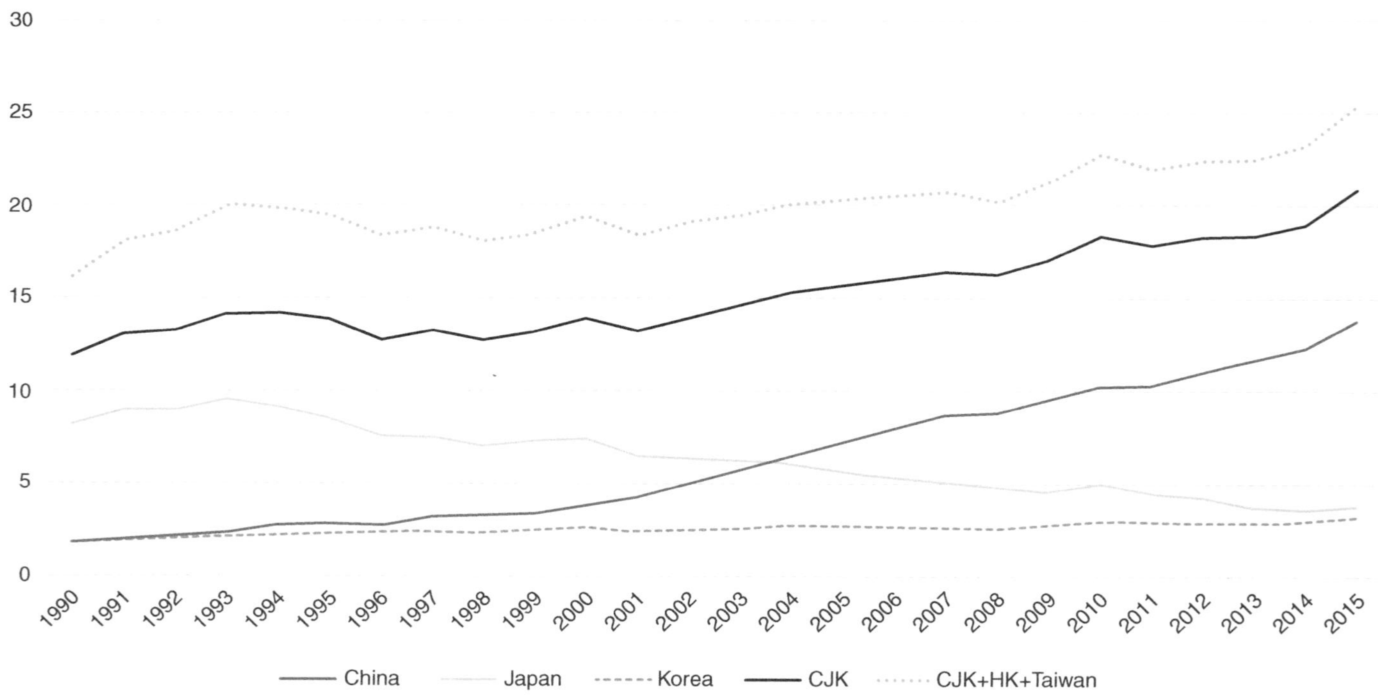

Figure 3.3 Share of CJK's exports in the world (%)

Source: WTO (2015), Statistics (accessed on 5 June 2016).

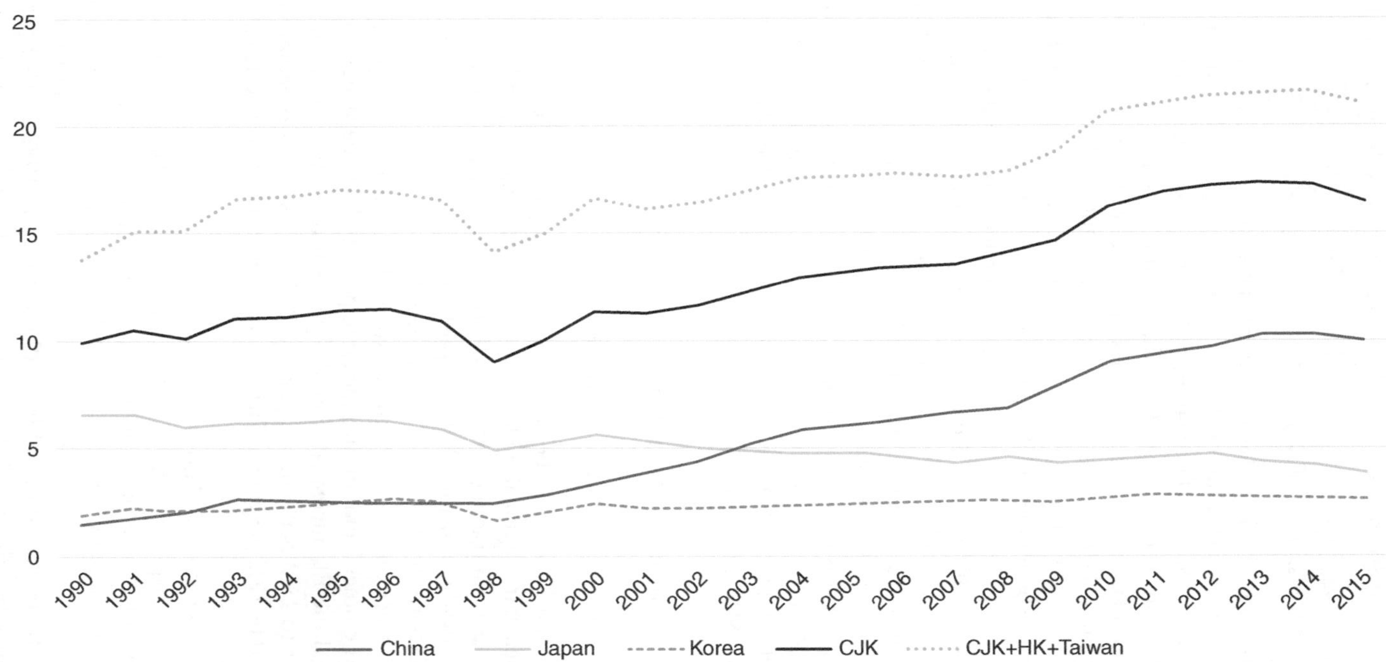

Figure 3.4 Share of CJK's imports in the world (%)

Source: WTO (2015), Statistics (accessed on 5 June 2016).

2003, respectively. Consequently, in 2015, the volumes of China's exports and imports represented 364 per cent and 259 per cent respectively, of those of Japan.

Foreign direct investment (FDI)

Compared to trade, the FDI flows of China, Japan and Korea differed significantly in many ways. First, inward FDI flows were considerably different from outward FDI flows. Second, fluctuations of FDI flows were much more volatile, and the FDI status in the world of the three countries was mostly lower. The share of inward FDI of the three countries increased from 3.1 per cent in 1990 to 14.0 per cent in 1994 before declining to 4.4 in 2000. This share continued to fluctuate, rising to 12.1 per cent in 2003 and diminishing again to 5.4 per cent in 2006 before rebounding to 11.4 per cent in 2014. As shown in Figure 3.5, in terms of inward FDI, China has been the most active of the three countries, whereas the shares of Japan and Korea have been considerably limited.

Regarding outward FDI flows, the global share of CJK, which represented 21.6 per cent in 1990, continued to diminish, dropping to 2.6 per cent in 1999 before increasing to 20.3 per cent in 2013; then 19.2 per cent in 2014. During this period, it was mostly Japan that occupied a dominant position. However, China's share of outward FDI flows has become substantial since 2005 and accounted for 8.6 per cent of the world total in 2014, surpassing that of Japan (8.4 per cent) (see Figure 3.6).

Functional economic integration in terms of trade

Major trade partners of China, Japan and Korea

China, Japan and Korea have become major trading partners for one another. However, their intra-regional trade dependency levels, export and import patterns, as well as main trading partners vary markedly. Japan and Korea used to be the major destination for China's exports until the mid-1990s. The share of China's exports to Japan-Korea rose rapidly from 1992 to 1996. After recording 25.4 per cent in 1996, these exports had fallen to 10.4 per cent by 2015.[11] On the other hand, during the same period, the trade shares (exports) of the US and the EU increased from 8.5 per cent to 18.0 per cent and from 10.7 per cent to 15.3 per cent respectively. ASEAN's share also became larger and amounted to 12.2 per cent in 2015, surpassing that of Japan-Korea in 2013 (see Figure 3.7).

Unlike China's exports to Japan and Korea, products from these two countries continued to be major imports for China. The share of Japan-Korea imports increased from 14.7 per cent in 1990 to 30.9 per cent in 1998 before declining to 19.8 per cent in 2015.[12] In addition, the EU has also been among China's major import partners; after having been more important than Japan-Korea in the early 1990s, its share dropped from 19.0 per cent in 1990 to 13.2 per cent in 2006 before recovering to 15.9 per cent in 2015. The US share declined from

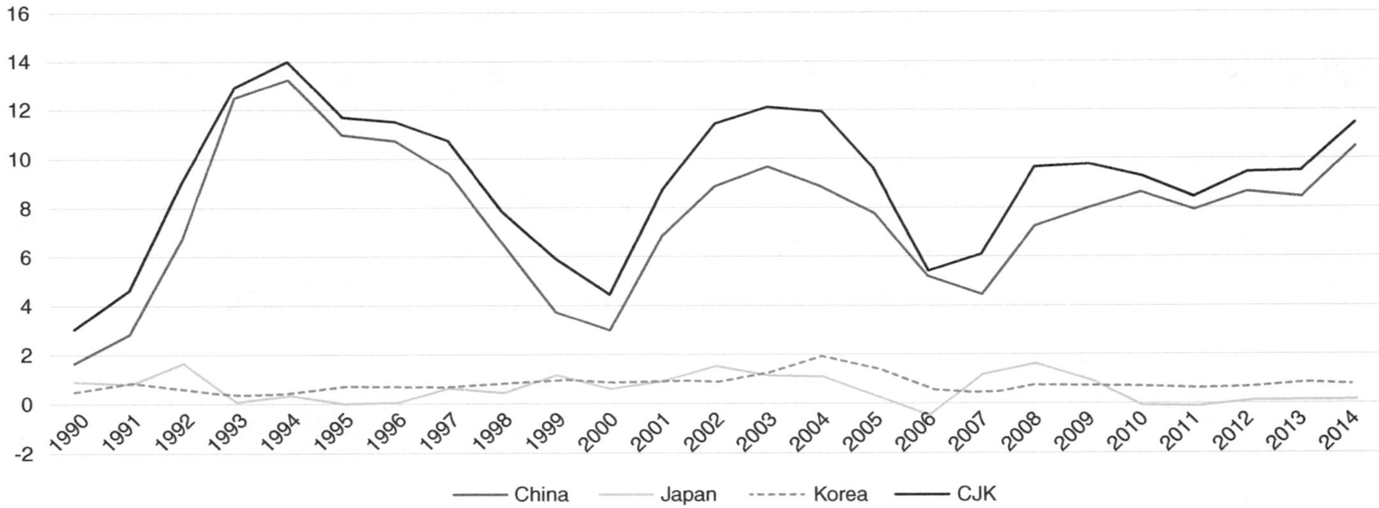

Figure 3.5 Share of CJK's inward FDIs in the world (%)

Source: UNCTAD (2015), Statistics (accessed on 20 June 2016).

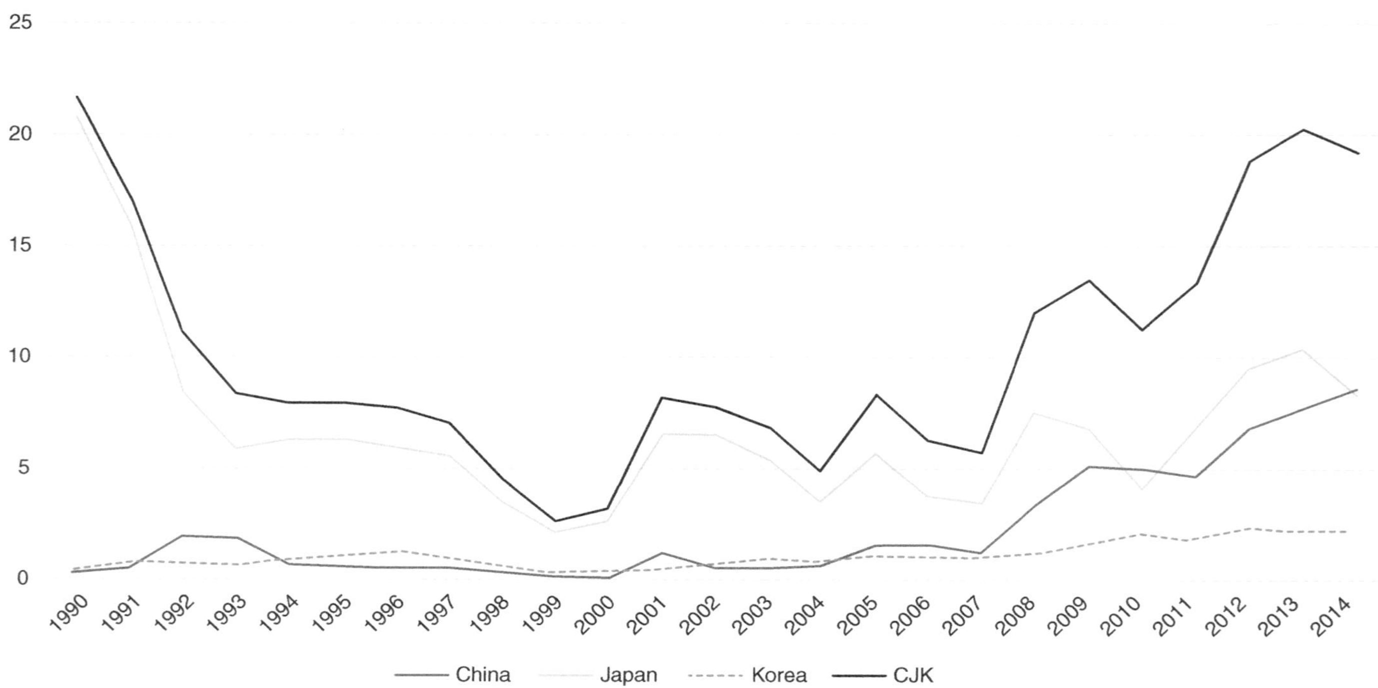

Figure 3.6 Share of CJK's outward FDIs in the world

Source: UNCTAD (2015), Statistics (accessed on 20 June 2016).

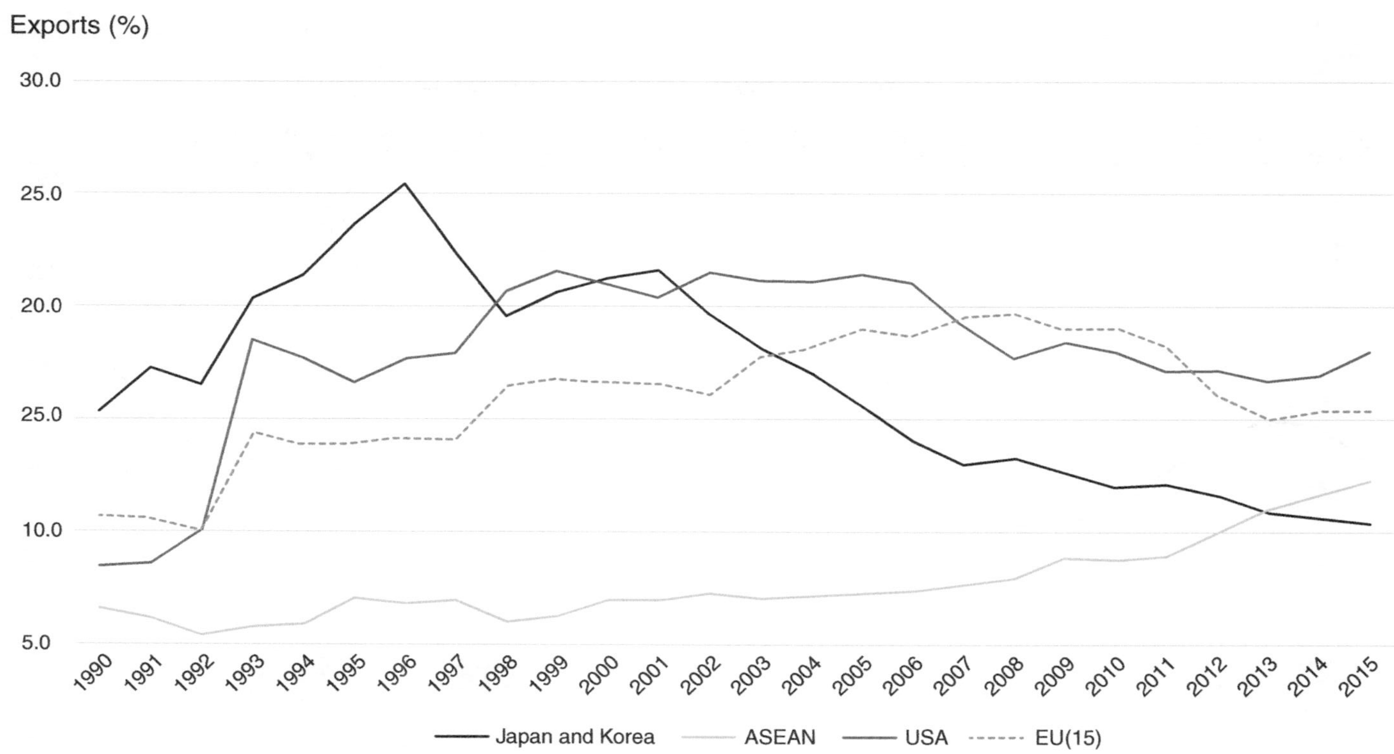

Figure 3.7 China's major trading partners

Source: IMF (2015), DOTS Database (accessed on 27 June 2016).

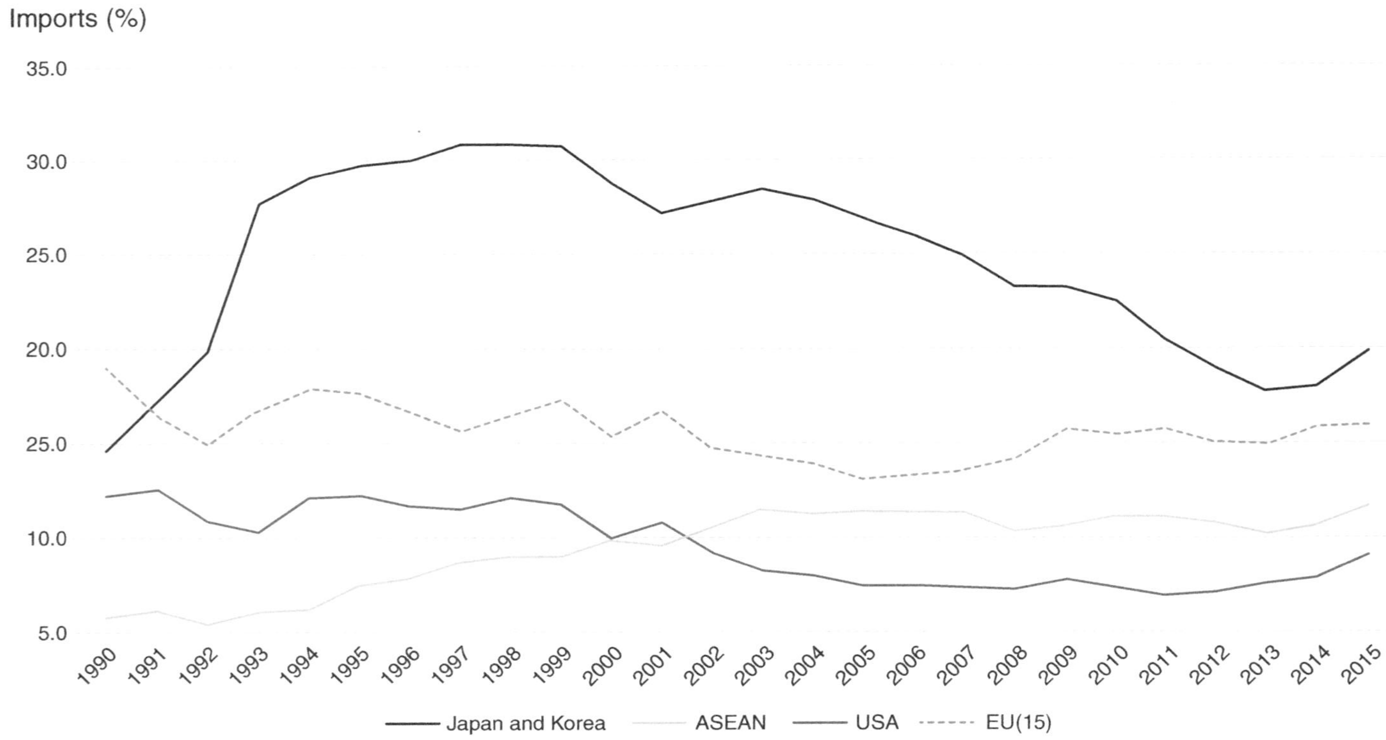

Figure 3.7 (Continued)

12.3 per cent to 9.0 per cent, while ASEAN's share has surpassed that of the US since 2002 and amounted to 11.6 per cent in 2015.

For Japan, the US used to be the most important export destination. However, China-Korea have become larger export partners for Japan than the US since 2007. Their share held by China-Korea surged from 8.2 per cent in 1990 to 27.7 per cent in 2011 before recording 24.5 per cent in 2015. Similarly, ASEAN has been a more important export partner for Japan than the EU since 2008 (see Figure 3.8).

The US was also Japan's major import partner in the 1990s. However, China-Korea have become more important than the US as an import partner for Japan since 2000. Their share soared from 10.1 per cent in 1990 to 28.9 per cent in 2015. In addition, ASEAN has become a more important import source for Japan, overtaking the US in 2004 and the EU has become a larger import partner than the US for Japan since 2011. For the period 1990–2015, the share represented by China-Japan in Korea's exports rose from 18.6 per cent to 30.9 per cent, while the share of the US in Korea's exports decreased from 28.6 per cent to 13.3 per cent. Thus, China-Japan have become the most important destination for Korea's exports since 1995. During the same period, the EU's share diminished from 14.2 per cent to 6.5 per cent, whereas ASEAN's share increased from 7.5 per cent to 14.2 per cent (see Figure 3.9).

With regard to Korea's imports, China-Japan have continued to occupy the dominant position over the past twenty-five years. The share represented by China-Japan fluctuated from 25.0 per cent in 1990 to 31.2 per cent in 2015. During the same period, the share of the US shrank from 22.8 per cent to 10.1 per cent, while that of ASEAN rose from 6.8 per cent to 10.3 per cent. On the other hand, the EU's share in Korea's imports remained relatively stable.

Bilateral trade dependencies between China, Japan and Korea

Whilst overall the bilateral trade trends among CJK for the period 1990–2015 have shown growth, it varied significantly between these countries. China-Korea trade has increased most rapidly, whereas Japan-Korea trade has grown much more slowly. Figure 3.10 shows that the declining share of intra-regional exports (Japan-Korea) in China's exports after reaching 25.4 per cent in 1996, was mainly due to a gradual decline of exports to Japan, whereas exports to Korea remained strong. Japan's share of China's exports increased from 14.7 per cent in 1990 to 20.4 per cent in 1996 before shrinking to 6.0 per cent in 2015, while Korea's share increased from 0.7 per cent to 4.5 per cent.

China's imports from Japan rose from 14.2 per cent in 1990 to 22.8 per cent in 1994 before falling continuously to 9.0 per cent in 2015. In contrast, imports from Korea increased from 0.4 per cent in 1990 to 10.7 per cent in 1998 and remained at similar levels until 2015, when they were recorded at 10.9 per cent. Thus, by 2013 Korea's share of China's imports had surpassed that of Japan.

In contrast, the share of Japan's intra-regional exports to China-Korea continued to increase until 2013 before diminishing somewhat to 24.5 per cent in 2015. As shown in Figure 3.11, this rise reflected mainly that of China's share

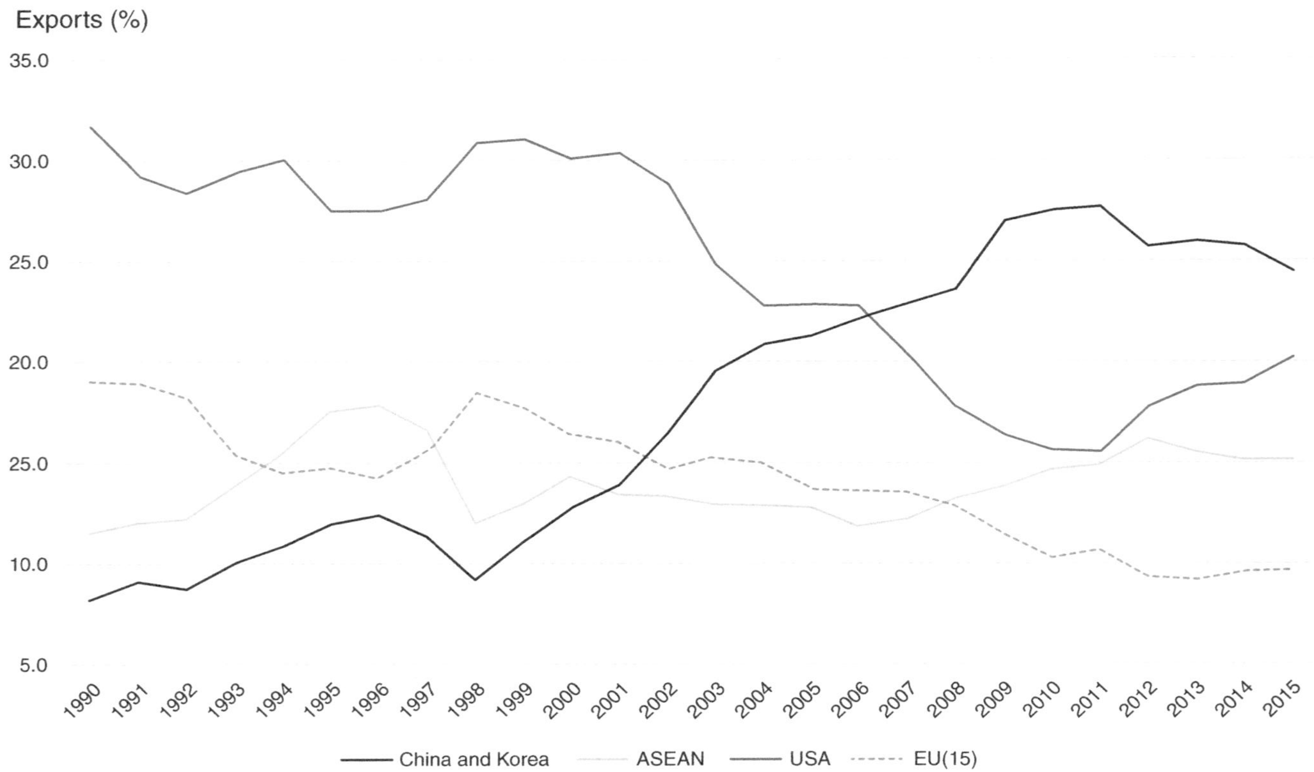

Exports (%)
35.0
30.0
25.0
20.0
25.0
10.0
5.0
1990
1991
1992
1993
1994
1995
1996
1997
1998
1999
2000
2001
2002
2003
2004
2005
2006
2007
2008
2009
2010
2011
2012
2013
2014
2015
China and Korea
ASEAN
USA
EU(15)

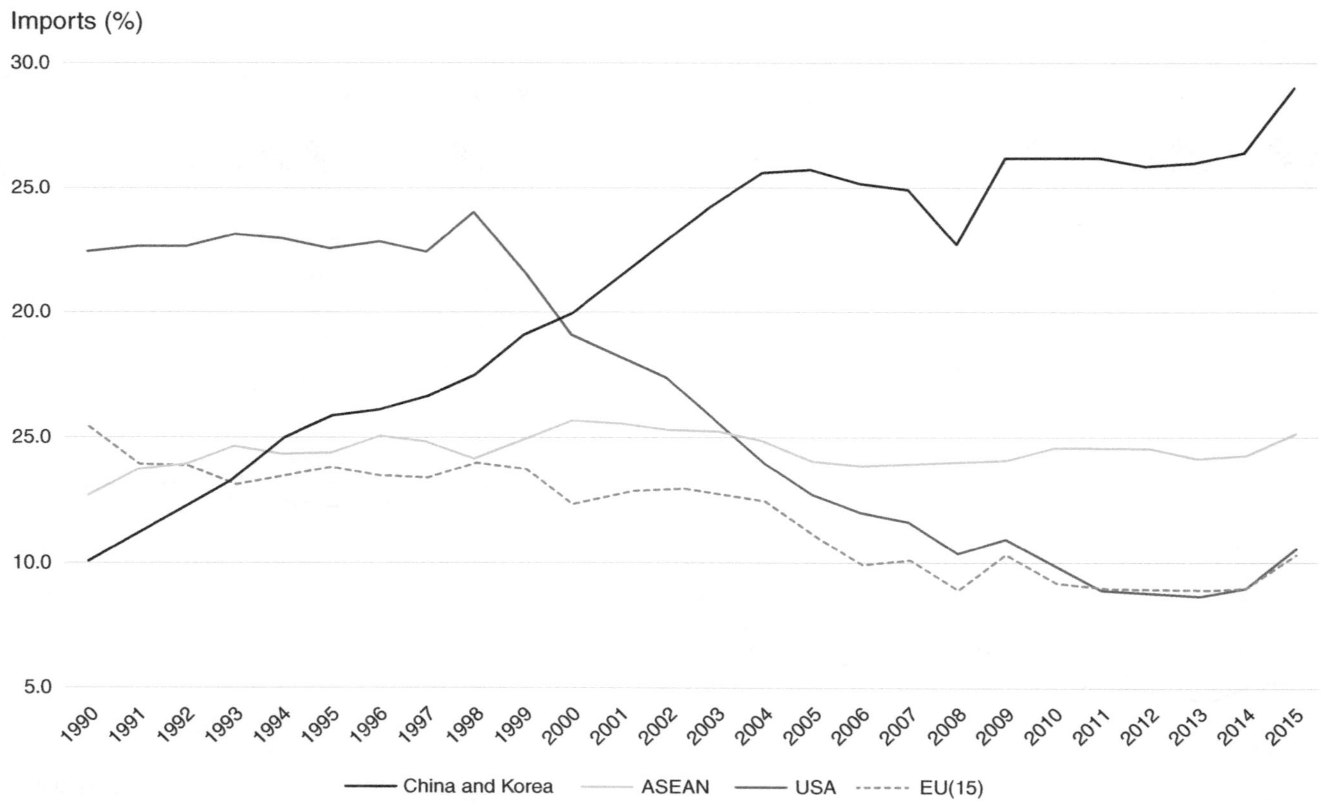

Figure 3.8 Japan's major trading partners

Source: IMF (2015), DOTS Database (accessed on 27 June 2016).

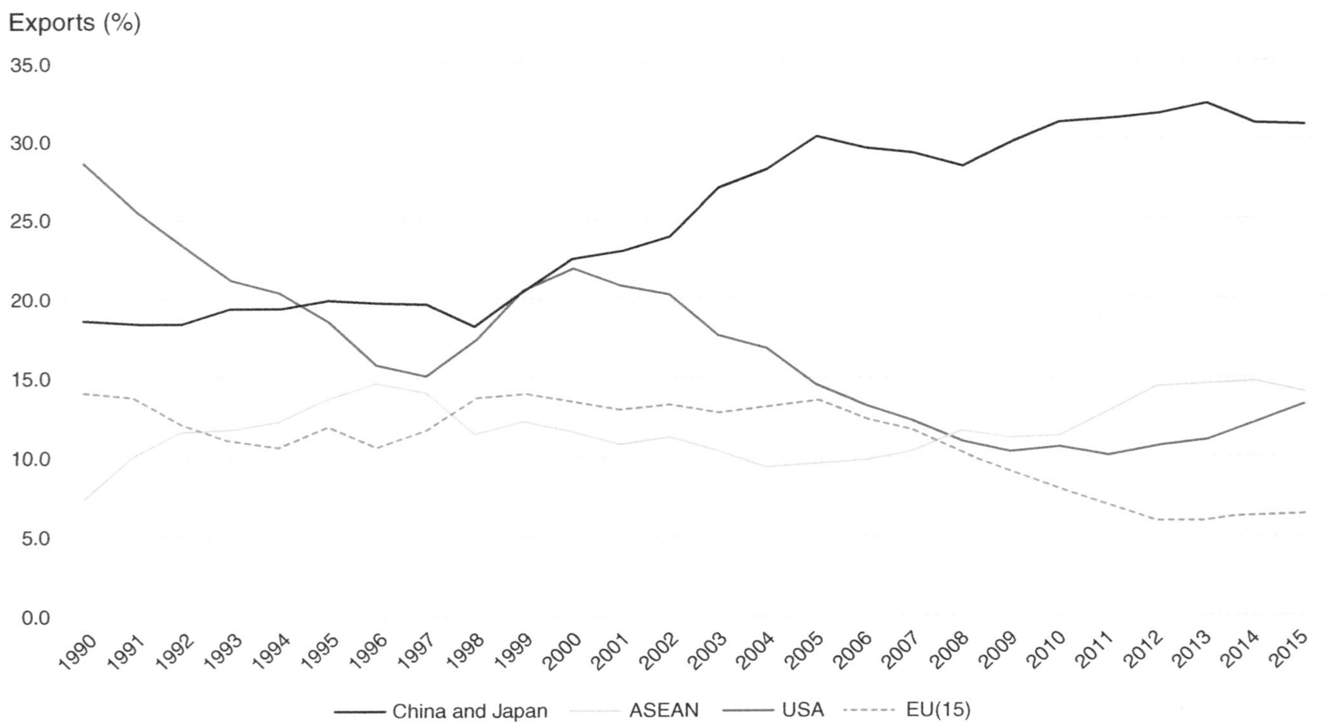

Exports (%)
35.0
30.0
25.0
20.0
15.0
10.0
5.0
0.0
1990
1991
1992
1993
1994
1995
1996
1997
1998
1999
2000
2001
2002
2003
2004
2005
2006
2007
2008
2009
2010
2011
2012
2013
2014
2015
China and Japan
ASEAN
USA
EU(15)

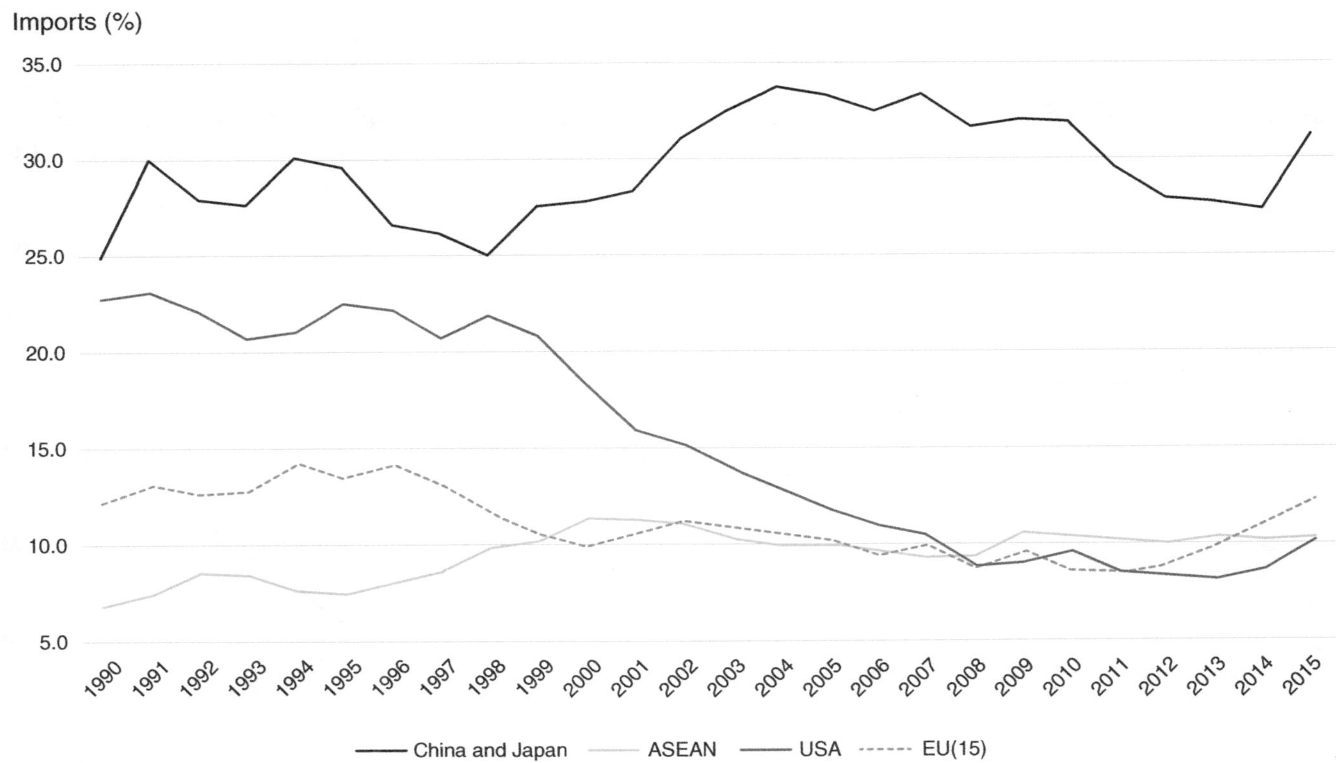

Figure 3.9 Korea's major trading partners

Source: IMF (2015), DOTS Database (accessed on 27 June 2016).

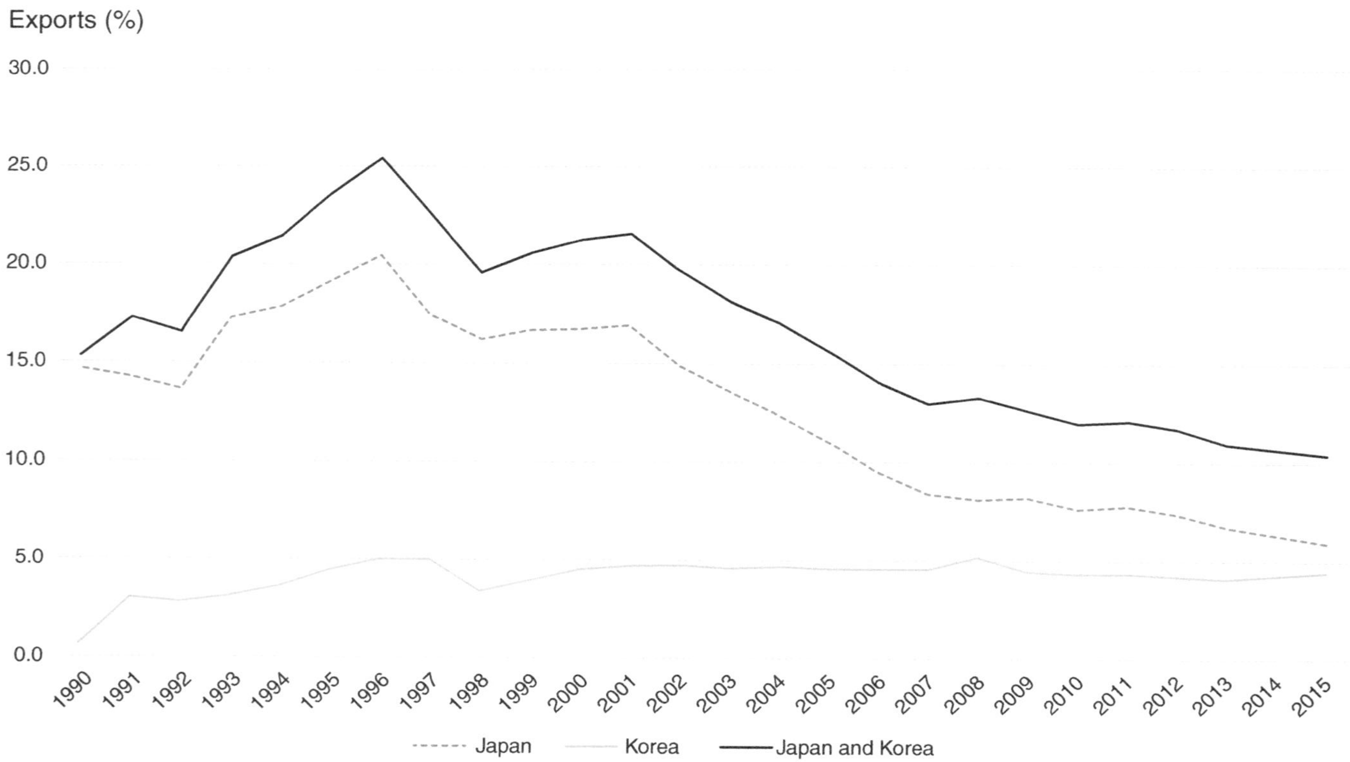

Exports (%)
30.0
25.0
20.0
15.0
10.0
5.0
0.0
1990
1991
1992
1993
1994
1995
1996
1997
1998
1999
2000
2001
2002
2003
2004
2005
2006
2007
2008
2009
2010
2011
2012
2013
2014
2015
Japan
Korea
Japan and Korea

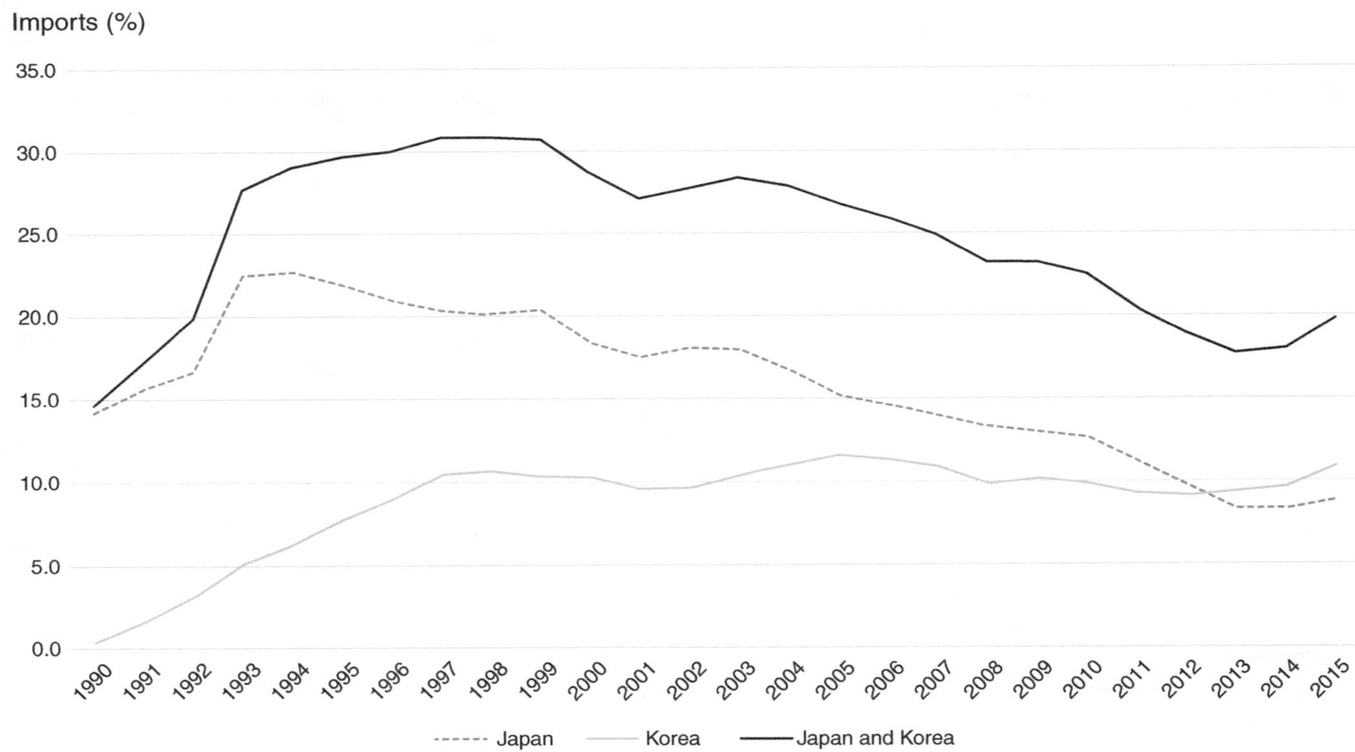

Figure 3.10 China's intra-regional trade

Source: IMF (2015), DOTS Database (accessed on 27 June 2016).

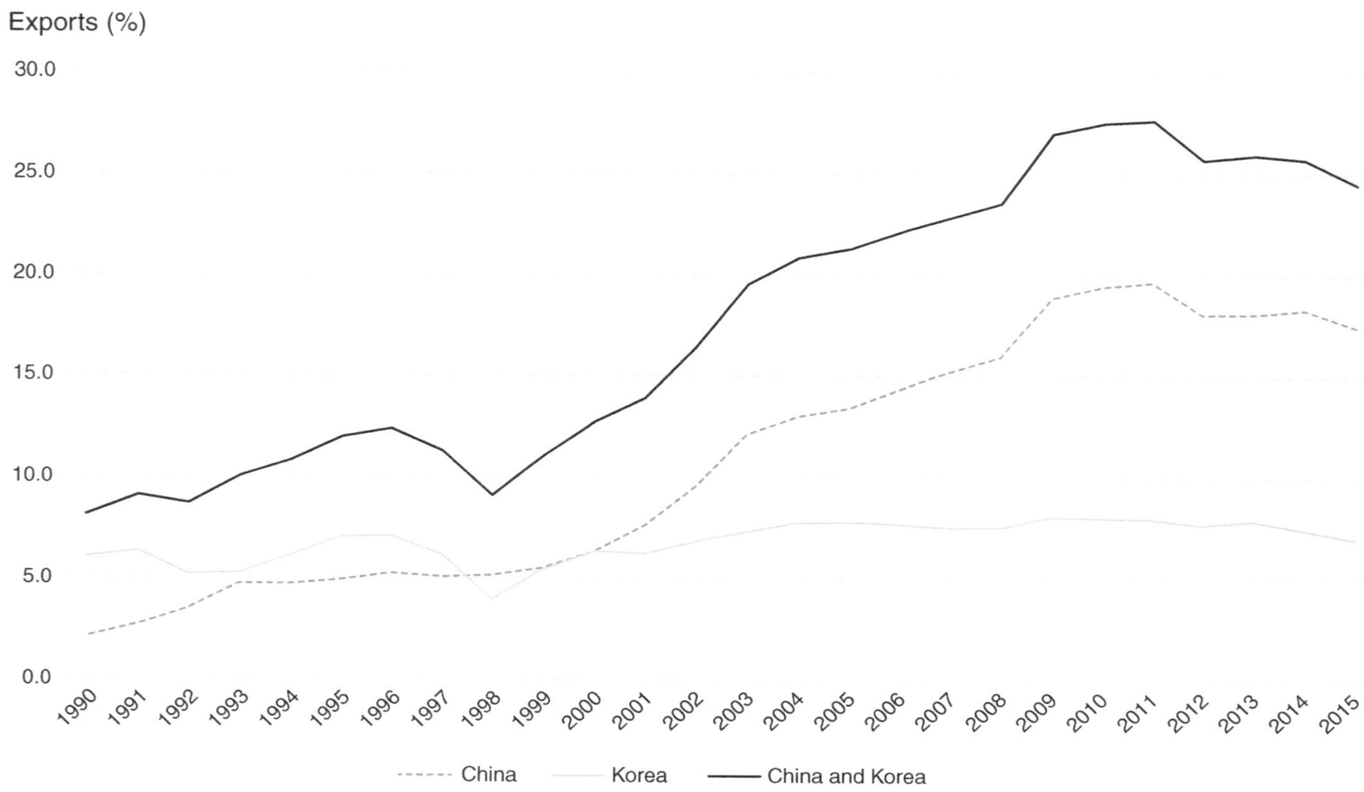

Exports (%)
30.0
25.0
20.0
15.0
10.0
5.0
0.0
1990
1991
1992
1993
1994
1995
1996
1997
1998
1999
2000
2001
2002
2003
2004
2005
2006
2007
2008
2009
2010
2011
2012
2013
2014
2015
China
Korea
China and Korea

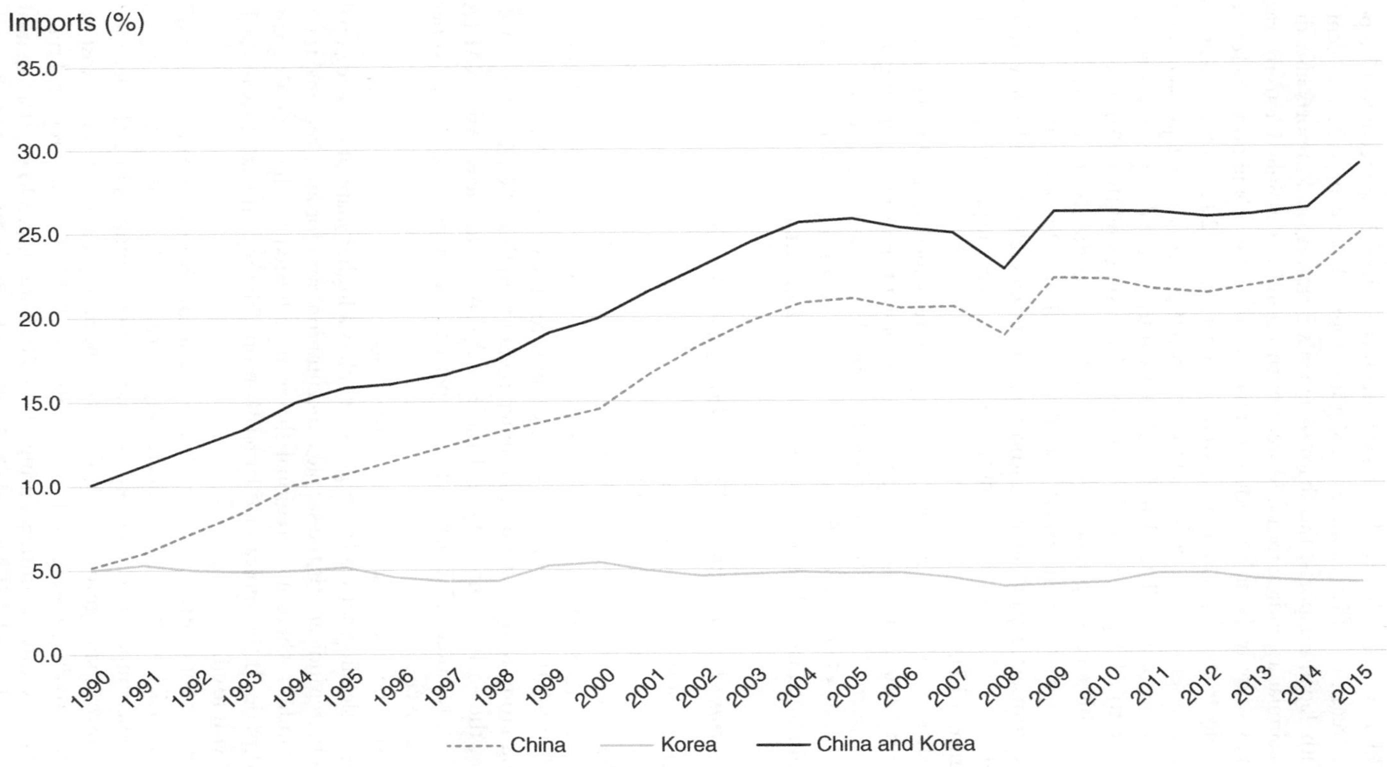

Figure 3.11 Japan's intra-regional trade

Source: IMF (2015), DOTS Database (accessed on 27 June 2016).

in Japan's exports, while Korea's share was relatively stable. During the period 1990–2015, China's share of Japan's exports surged from 2.1 per cent to 17.5 per cent, whereas that of Korea increased slightly from 6.1 per cent to 7.0 per cent.

As with Japan's exports, the share of Japan's intra-regional imports also displayed a similar ascending trend. Moreover, this trend was mainly due to the rise of China's share in Japan's imports. China's share in Japan's imports increased dramatically from 5.1 per cent in 1990 to 25.8 per cent in 2015, whereas Korea's share in Japan's imports declined slowly from 5.0 per cent to 4.1 per cent during the same period. The share of Korea's intra-regional exports continued to increase to 31.1 per cent in 2013 before decreasing slightly to 30.9 per cent in 2015. This ascending tendency was mainly due to the rise of China's share in Korea's exports, which surged from 0.9 per cent in 1990 to 26.0 per cent in 2015. In contrast, Japan's share in Korea's exports generally showed a downward trend, shrinking from 19.4 per cent to 4.9 per cent over the past twenty-five years (see Figure 3.12).

The share of Korea's intra-regional imports remained relatively stable over the period 1990–2015, oscillating around 30 per cent. However, with regard to Korea's exports, China's and Japan's share moved in opposite directions: China's share in Korea's imports rose from 3.2 per cent to 20.7 per cent, whereas Japan's share continued to decline from 26.6 per cent to 10.5 per cent.

Intra-regional trade between China, Japan and Korea

In general, the share of intra-regional trade in the overall trade between China, Japan and Korea increased until 2004, reaching 24.1 per cent before diminishing gradually to 19.5 per cent in 2015. As shown in Figure 3.13, the share has been lower than that of ASEAN, not to mention the EU and NAFTA throughout the period 1990–2015. However, the share of intra-regional trade of Northeast Asia including Hong Kong and Taiwan is much higher than that of CJK and ASEAN. In 2015, the share of intra-regional trade of ASEAN, Northeast Asia, NAFTA and EU represented 23.7 per cent, 34.8 per cent, 41.1 per cent and 52.6 per cent respectively.

However, the comparison across regions based on share of intra-regional trade could be misleading since a larger group exhibits a higher share of intra-regional trade. A better indicator is the simple concentration ratio (or intra-regional trade intensity index) where intra-regional shares are adjusted by the region's share in world trade. If this indicator is larger than one, the region has a bias towards trading with itself.

The simple concentration ratio of China, Japan and Korea increased from 1.07 in 1990 to 1.71 in 2003 before decreasing to 1.04 in 2015. It is interesting to note that the simple concentration ratio of the three countries in 2015 declined to levels lower than figures recorded in 1990, meaning that there was almost no bias towards trading among the three countries in 2015. The intra-regional trade intensity of the three countries during 1990–2015 was much lower than that of the EU, NAFTA and ASEAN; only in 1998 and between 2001 and 2004 was it

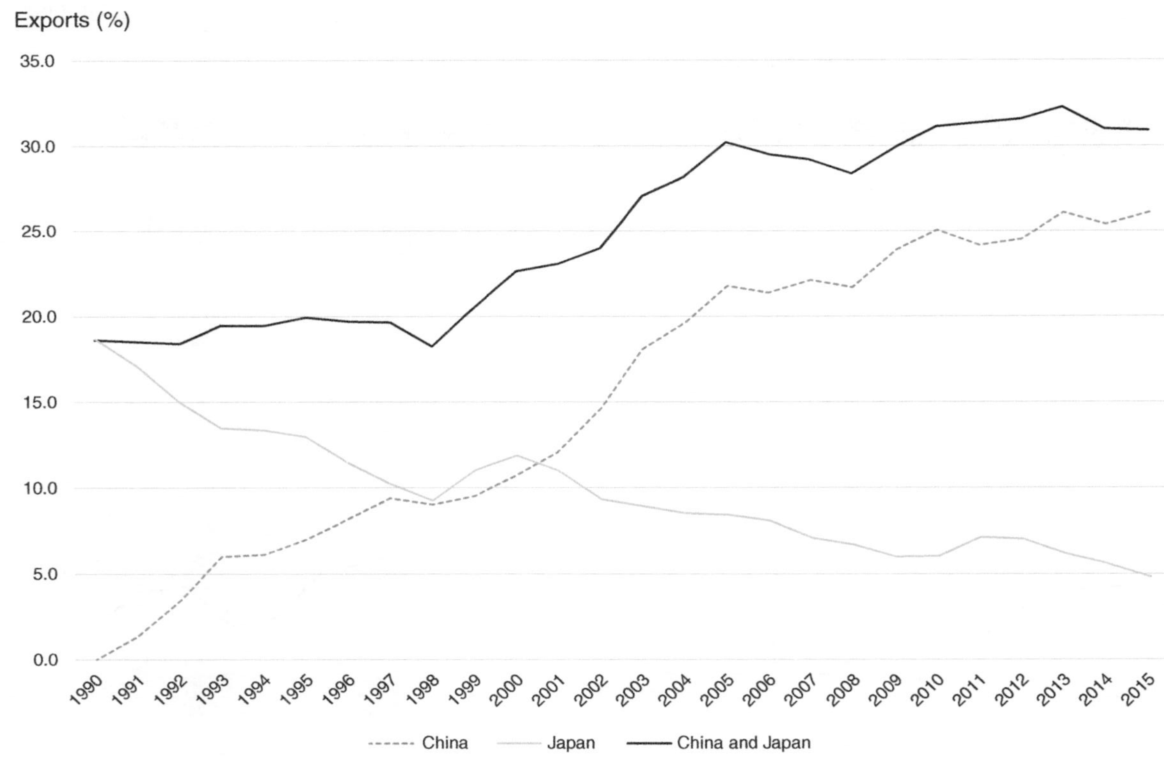

Figure 3.12 Korea's intra-regional trade

Source: IMF (2015), DOTS Database (accessed on 27 June 2016).

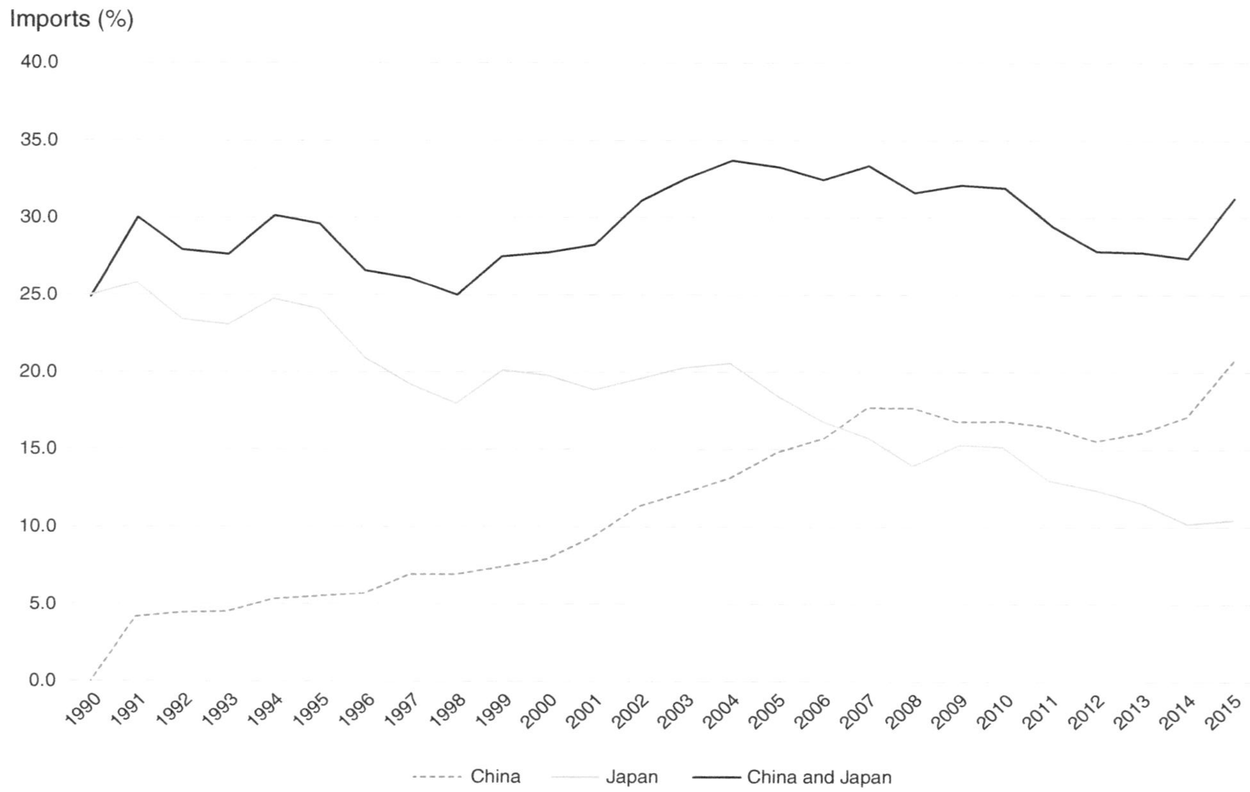

Figure 3.12 (Continued)

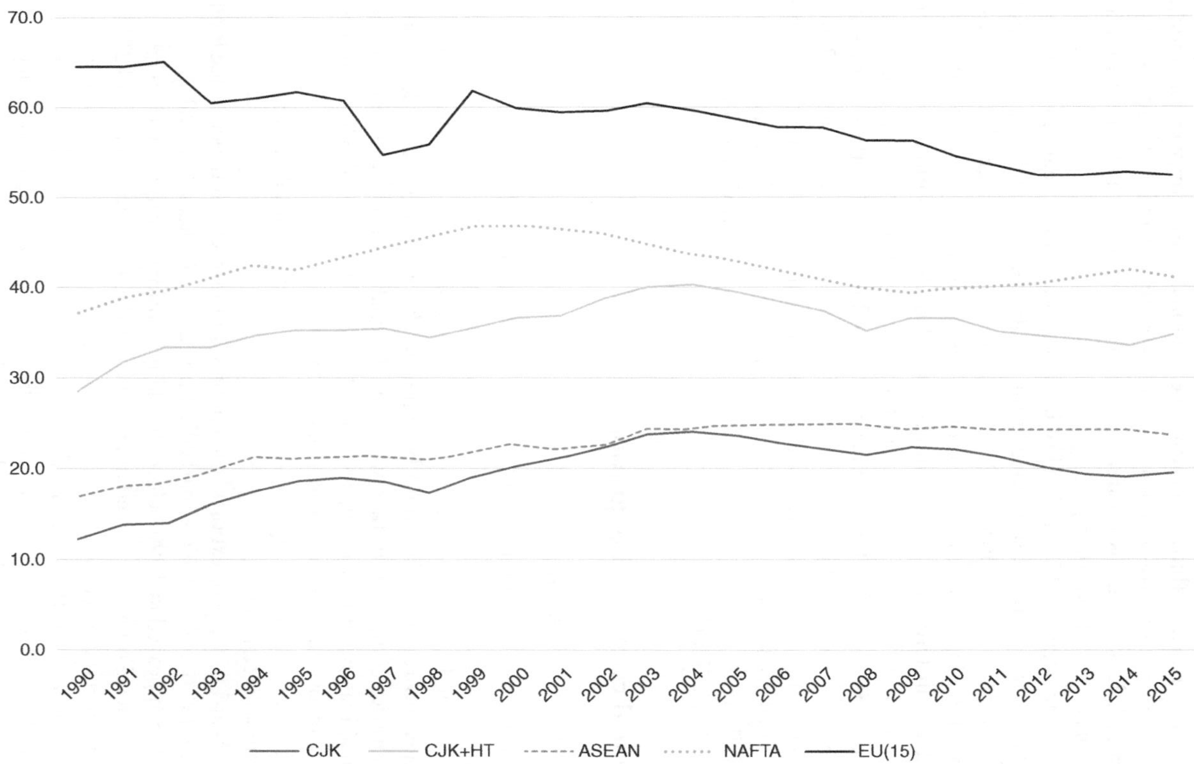

Figure 3.13 Shares of intra-regional trade

Source: Calculated from IMF (2015), DOTS Database; Taiwan Bureau of Foreign Trade, Trade Statistic (accessed on 30 June 2016).

slightly higher than that of the EU (see Figure 3.14). In 2015, simple concentration ratios of the EU, NAFTA and ASEAN represented 1.88, 2.48 and 3.33 respectively.

This simple concentration ratio also has a weakness in that it considers only internal bias. Thus, a third indicator, the regional trade introversion index, which considers both intra-regional bias and extra-regional bias of trade, should be measured. If the index is greater than zero, the region's trade has an intra-regional bias (Hamanaka 2015).

As shown in Figure 3.15, the level of intra-regional trade integration between China, Japan and Korea rose gradually until 2003 before falling steadily until 2014 and rebounding a little in 2015. Furthermore, considerable gaps exist between China-Japan-Korea and the other groups including ASEAN, the EU and NAFTA, in terms of levels of intra-regional trade integration. On the one hand, the regional introversion index of the three countries increased from 0.04 in 1990 to 0.38 in 2003 before diminishing to 0.03 in 2015. On the other hand, during the same period, the index of other regions fluctuated between 0.52 and 0.74. According to the regional trade introversion index, there was almost no intra-regional trade bias (0.03) among the three Northeast Asian countries in 2015, while high intra-regional trade biases existed in ASEAN (0.67), the EU (0.66) and NAFTA (0.68).

Functional economic integration

Trade between China, Japan and Korea

The level of economic integration between China, Japan and Korea in terms of trade increased from 1990 to 2003 before decreasing continuously until 2015. As a result, the level of integration in 2015 was similar to that of 1990, so low that almost no regional bias could be found in the intra-regional trade among these countries compared to trade with non-regional countries, while high levels of regional bias existed for countries of the EU, NAFTA and ASEAN. However, as shown in our analyses of export and import partners of China, Japan and Korea, the situation varied significantly at country level and bilateral trends differed from trilateral trends.

With regard to China's exports, the country's intra-regional dependency level peaked in 1996 before falling markedly until 2015. China's bilateral dependency on Japan peaked in 1999 before shrinking considerably until 2015, while its dependency level on Korea peaked in 2008 before declining gradually until 2015. China's imports showed a somewhat similar trend; its intra-regional dependency level peaked in 1998 before diminishing until 2015. Unlike its exports, China's imports level in 2015 was still substantial. Bilaterally, China's dependency level on Japan peaked in 1994 before falling precipitously until 2015, while its dependency level on Korea peaked in 2005, and held steady until 2015. Thus, from the Chinese perspective, the overall intra-regional trade dependency decreased after peaking in the second half of the 1990s. This decline was mainly

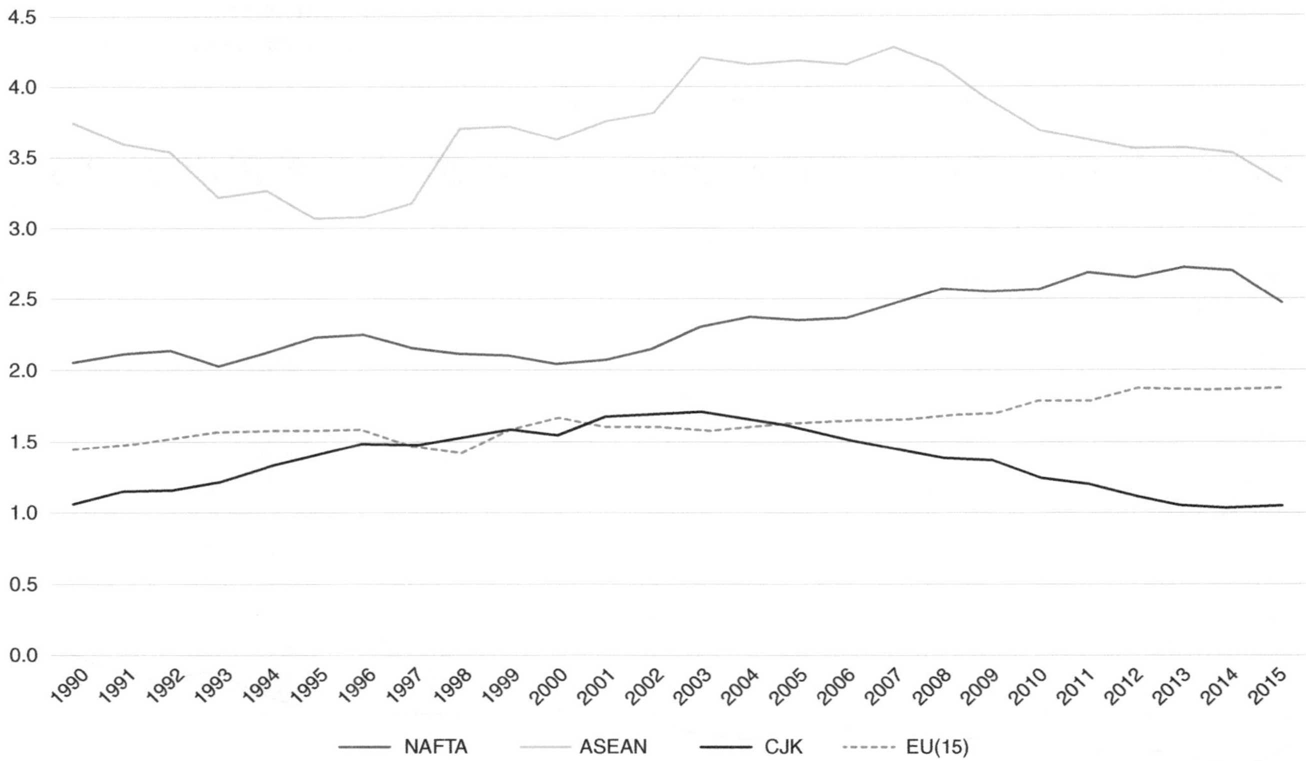

Figure 3.14 Simple concentration ratios

Source: Calculated from IMF (2015), DOTS Database (accessed on 27 June 2016).

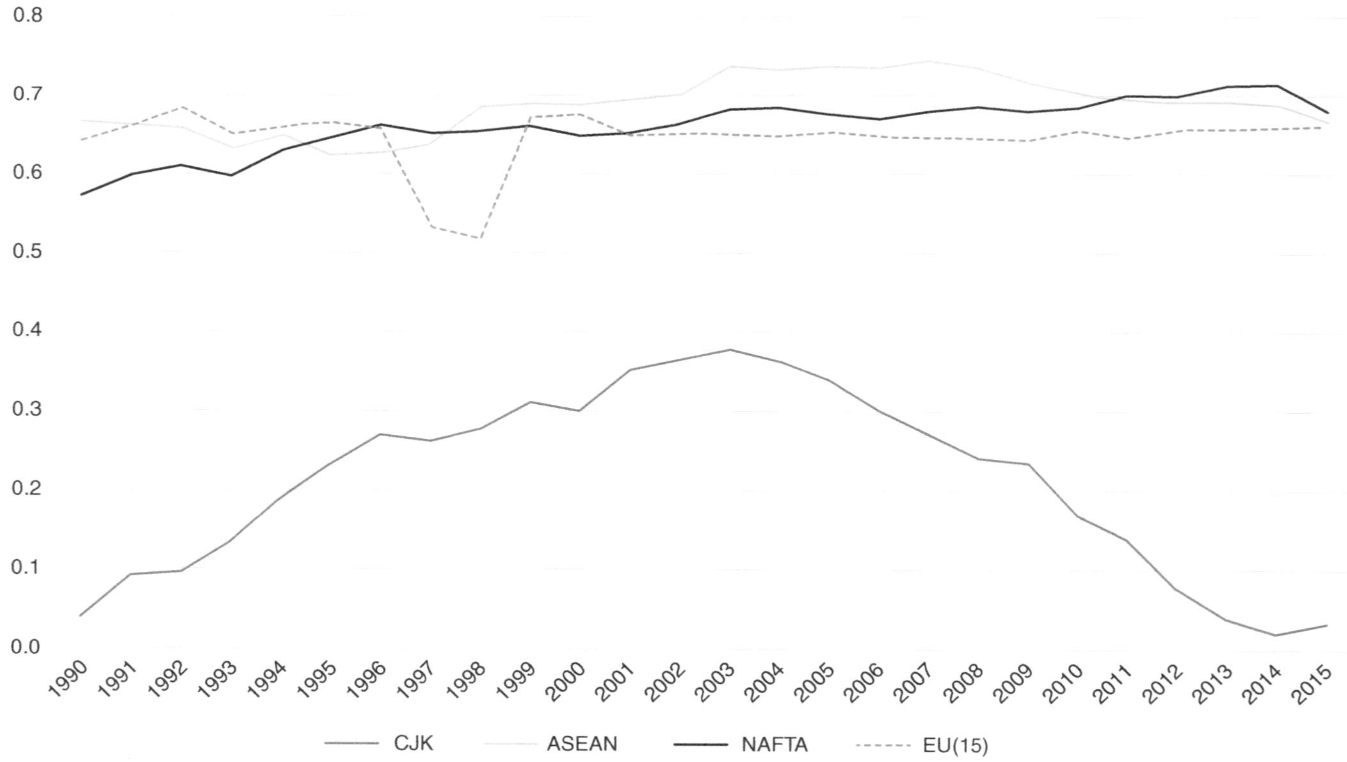

Figure 3.15 Regional introversion index

Source: Calculated from IMF (2015), DOTS Database (accessed on 27 June 2016).

due to weakening trade dependency on Japan, while trade dependency on Korea remained relatively strong, although it weakened slightly after peaking in the second half of the 2000s.

With reference to Japan's exports, its intra-regional dependency level rose until 2011 and remained strong until 2015. Bilaterally, Japan's dependency level on China peaked in 2011, and remained high until 2015, while its dependency level on Korea peaked in 2009, and remained at a similar level until 2015. Japan's imports situation is unique in that the country's intra-regional dependency level continued to rise until 2015. Bilaterally, its dependency level on China also continued to increase until 2015, whereas its dependency level on Korea peaked in 2000 before diminishing until 2015. In contrast to the Chinese perspective, Japan's overall intra-regional trade dependency has increased significantly over the past twenty-five years. This surge occurred due to its growing trade dependency on China, whereas its trade dependency level on Korea fluctuated over the same period.

Korea's intra-regional export dependency level increased until 2013 and remained strong until 2015. Bilaterally, Korea's dependency level on China peaked in 2013, and remained high until 2015, while its dependency level on Japan has continued to fall over the past twenty-five years. In contrast to its exports, Korea's intra-regional imports dependency level remained consistently high over the past twenty-five years peaking in 2004. Bilaterally, Korea's dependency level on China continued to rise until 2015, while its dependency level on Japan continued to fall until 2015, even though its level in 2015 remained substantial. Korea's overall intra-regional trade dependency increased over the past twenty-five years. Since 2015, the country's intra-regional trade dependency level has been the highest among the three countries, mainly due to its growing trade dependency on China, whereas its trade dependency level on Japan continued to decline over this period.

In short, after having risen during the first half of the past twenty-five years, the level of economic integration in terms of trade among the three above-mentioned countries steadily declined during the second half. This decline was mainly caused by China's decreasing trade dependency on Japan and to a lesser degree by a decrease in Korea's trade dependency on Japan. Chinese predominance in intra-regional trade trends reflects the overriding scale of its economy and trade. On the other hand, the intra-regional trade dependency of Japan and Korea increased during the same period, once again, due mainly to their growing trade dependency on China.

Investment between China, Japan and Korea

As mentioned earlier, the overall FDI status of China, Japan and Korea in the world has been much less important than that of trade. Country-wise, China has occupied a predominant position among the three countries in inward FDI flows, whereas, in terms of outward FDI flows, Japan has maintained a dominant position even though its position was threatened recently by the growing importance of China. With respect to China's inward FDI flows, Hong Kong has been by far the most important partner representing 53.5 per cent in 1995 and 68.4 per cent in 2015. Japan and Korea were also significant partners in the mid-2000s, but their relative importance gradually diminished. The Japan-Korea trade share rose from 11.1 per cent in 1990 to 19.3 per cent in 2004 before shrinking to 5.7 per cent in 2015. Japan's share increased 8.3 per cent in 1995 to 9.6 per cent in 1997 before declining to 2.5 per cent in 2015, while Korea's share rose from 2.8 per cent in 1995 to 10.3 per cent in 2004 before diminishing to 3.2 per cent in 2015 (see Figure 3.16).

Hong Kong occupied the most dominant position in China's outward FDI flows, accounting for more than half of the total flow since the mid-2000s. In contrast, the roles of Japan and Korea were very limited. For example, in 2014, the shares of Japan and Korea in China's outward FDI flows amounted to a mere 0.3 per cent and 0.5 per cent respectively, whereas those of the EU and US represented 8.8 per cent and 6.2 per cent respectively.[13]As mentioned earlier, the levels of Japan's inward FDI flows have been very low. In addition, the role of China and Korea in Japan's inward FDI has been limited. In 2014, the share of China and Korea was 4.2 per cent and 3.0 per cent respectively, while that of the US and the EU represented 37.1 per cent and 14.7 per cent respectively.[14] In contrast to Japan's inward FDI flows, its outward FDI flows have been substantial. Moreover, China and to a lesser extent Korea, have been a somewhat important destination for Japan's outward FDI. The China-Korea share in Japan's outward FDI rose from 0.85 per cent in 1990 to 21.4 per cent in 2004 before diminishing to 8.1 per cent in 2015. The US and EU have been major destinations for Japan's outward FDI, and since 2013, ASEAN countries have become a more important destination than China-Korea (see Figure 3.17).

The US and the EU have been the major sources of Korea's inward FDI over the past twenty-five years. Japan had also been an important source until recently, while China has emerged as a new source only recently. As a result, China's share (9.5 per cent) in Korea's inward FDI flows surpassed that of Japan (8.0 per cent) for the first time in 2015.[15] With respect to Korea's outward FDI, China has been an important destination. China's share increased from 2.4 per cent in 1990 to 44.3 per cent in 2003 before shrinking to 10.7 per cent in 2015. In contrast, Japan's share had been quite low before rising to 4.5 per cent in 2015. In addition, the US, EU and ASEAN have been major destinations of Korea's outward FDI.[16]

To summarize, in terms of investment, the level of intra-regional economic integration among the three Northeast Asian countries has been much lower compared to the level of trade integration. Among the FDI flows, the most meaningful flows related to the three countries were China's inward FDI flows and Japan's outward FDI flows. Although Japan and Korea were important players for China's inward FDI flows in the mid-2000s, they have become much less important in recent years. Similarly, China was one of the major destinations for Japan's outward FDI flows in the mid-2000s and early-2010s but has recently become less important compared to the US, EU and ASEAN.

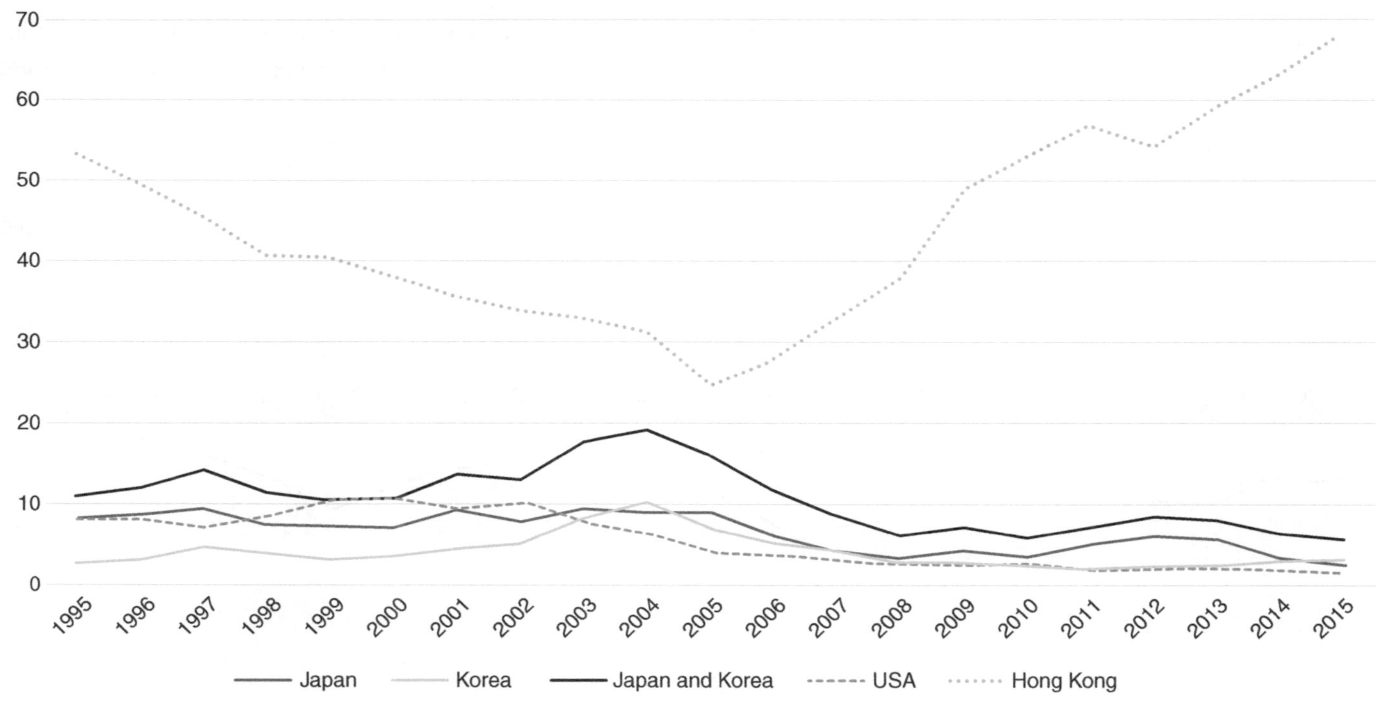

Figure 3.16 China's inward FDI flows (%)

Source: CEIC (2015), China Premium Database (accessed on 15 June 2016).

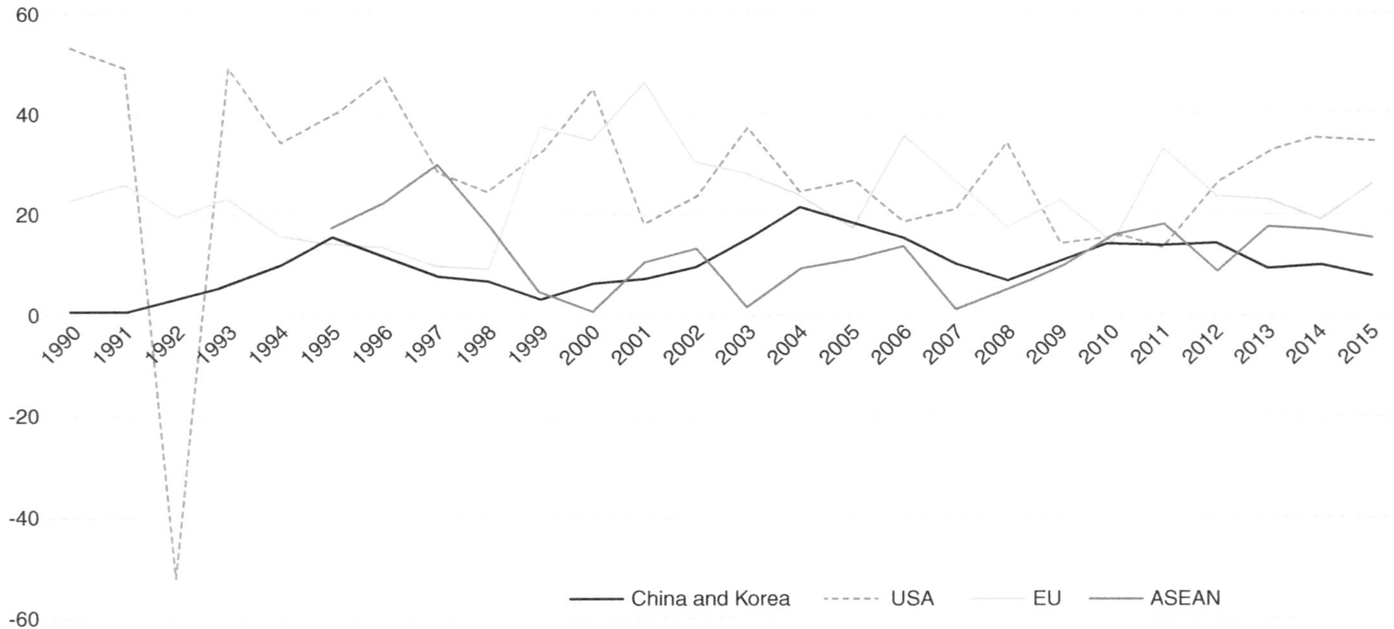

Figure 3.17 Japan's outward FDI flows (%)

Source: JETRO (2015), Japanese Trade and Investment Statistics (accessed on 15 June 2016).

Conclusion

This chapter has outlined and analysed the degree of functional economic integration between China, Japan and Korea. Clearly there is considerable trade and investment between CJK, although this has fluctuated from time to time. The size of the CJK market, the complementary nature of the individual economies and geographical proximity all point to a strong economic argument for a CJK FTA which would not only benefit the three countries but also contribute greatly to the economic prosperity of East Asia. There are, however, serious obstacles to such integration as will be seen in the following chapter, and the delays that have occurred in institutional building that would guide and facilitate the economic integration of Northeast Asia.

Notes

1 Sohn (1995). The linear model of economic integration is described as a sequential process of economic integration that allows the members the discretion to proceed at their own pace.
2 Sometimes this also includes Inner Mongolia and even the maritime regions of China, which are to the north of Shanghai.
3 The Olympic Model, which emphasizes the multi-layered character of Northeast Asian economic cooperation, can be regarded as an attempt to conceptualize Northeast Asian economic cooperation not as local integration but as comprehensive economic cooperation (Lee 1996).
4 The TRADP evolved into the Greater Tumen Initiative (GTI) extending the territory from the initial triangle areas around the Tumen River area to a more extensive area including China, Mongolia, Russia and South Korea. In 2009, GTI became a member-driven cooperation mechanism and member countries established the rotation system for Chair and Chair Country, while DPRK (North Korea) withdrew from GTI. The process of transforming the GTI into an independent legal entity started in 2010. Most recently, the sixteenth GTI Consultative Committee Meeting was held in Seoul on 28 April 2016. However, no significant progress was made mainly because of the different views between China and Russia over naming the organization.
5 In order to prevent the spread of crisis from one country to another, East Asian countries felt the need to reinforce regional economic cooperation. At present, there is more action in the area of financial cooperation rather than trade cooperation through the creation of an economic cooperative body. Bilateral Swap Agreements (BSAs) are now in force in East Asian countries through the Chiang Mai Initiative (CMI). Ahn and Cheong (2007) argue that the CMI triggered by the 1997 Asian financial crisis should be a turning point towards regional integration as there is a critical need for CJK to establish a formal institution that would allow "mutual consultation regarding exchange rates, interest rates and foreign exchange reserves" (Ahn and Cheong 2007: 178). A key function of the CMI is to promptly provide liquidity assistance such as monitoring, surveillance and exchange rate coordination to regional countries showing signs of a currency crisis by equipping and strengthening liquidity assistance facilities (Kawai 2005).
6 When Hong Kong and Taiwan are included, Northeast Asia's share rose from 17.3 per cent to 23.7 per cent during the same period.
7 If Hong Kong and Taiwan are added, Northeast Asia's share of exports increased from 16.2 per cent to 25.4 per cent during the same period.

8 It is worth noting that the CJK share of GDP in the world continued to increase even in 2015 when the volume of their exports shrank.
9 When Hong and Taiwan are added, Northeast Asia's share of imports increased from 13.8 per cent to 21.0 per cent during the same period.
10 However, unlike exports, the share of imports of the three countries decreased in 2014–2015 after recording 17.4 per cent in 2013.
11 Although Northeast Asia including Hong Kong and Taiwan continues to be the most important export destination, their share has also declined from 46.5 per cent in 1990 to 28.2 per cent in 2015.
12 The share of Northeast Asia including Hong Kong and Taiwan decreased from 46.5 per cent in 1990 to 28.2 per cent in 2015.
13 CEIC, China Premium Database (accessed on 15 June 2016).
14 JETRO, Japanese Trade and Investment Statistics (accessed on 15 June 2016).
15 Ministry of Trade, Industry and Energy, Republic of Korea, FDI statistics (accessed 15 June 2016).
16 The Export and Import Bank of Korea, Outward FDI statistics (accessed 15 June 2016).

4 Institutional building between China, Japan and Korea

Introduction

The institutional building process began in the context of East Asia in the wake of the Asian financial crisis. The first summit meeting was held among the leaders of ASEAN+3 countries (China, Japan and Korea) in Kuala Lumpur in December 1997. Summit meetings have since taken place regularly and evolved into the ASEAN+3 framework. It was this ASEAN+3 framework that was instrumental in initiating the first mechanism related to institutional economic integration between China, Japan and Korea.

CJK institutional framework

Summit meetings

The leaders of the three countries at the time, namely Chinese Premier Zhu Rong-ji, Japanese Prime Minister Keizo Obuchi and Korea's President Kim Dae-jung, met for the first time in Manila on 28 November 1999 on the occasion of the ASEAN+3 Summit Meeting. At this historic meeting they agreed among other matters to launch a trilateral joint research project, to be carried out by research institutes in the three countries, on economic cooperation between China, Japan and Korea. The leaders of the three countries agreed in Singapore on 24 November 2000 to hold the Trilateral Summit Meetings regularly. The Trilateral Foreign Ministers' Meeting was created at the Bandar Seri Begawan Summit Meeting held on 5 November 2001, and the leaders agreed that the Economic and Trade Ministers' Meeting and the Finance Ministers' Meeting would take place regularly. At the Phnom Penh Summit Meeting on 4 November 2002, the leaders agreed on the formalization of the Trilateral Summit Meeting, and the first Business Forum was held.

The "Joint Declaration on the Promotion of Tripartite Cooperation among the People's Republic of China, Japan and the Republic of Korea" was adopted in Bali on 7 October 2003. According to the Joint Declaration, the scope of tripartite cooperation consisted of trade and investment, information and communication technology (ICT), environmental protection, disaster prevention and management, energy, finance, science and technology, tourism, fishery resource conservation, people-to-people exchange, culture, education and human resources development, news media, public health and sports, international affairs, Asian regional cooperation, exchange and cooperation among the defence and military personnel and prevention of infectious diseases and transnational crimes. Furthermore, in order to study, plan, coordinate and monitor the cooperation activities under way or envisaged by this Joint Declaration, the leaders decided to set up a three-party committee. The committee was to submit progress reports to the annual summit meeting.

The "Progress Report of the Trilateral Cooperation among People's Republic of China, Japan and the Republic of Korea" and "The Action Strategy on Trilateral Cooperation among the People's Republic of China, Japan and the Republic of Korea" were endorsed at the Vientiane Summit Meeting held on 29 November 2004. The Summit was not held in 2005 due to opposition to Japan's Prime Minister Koizumi's visit to Yasukuni Shrine, and the next meeting took place in Cebu on 14 January 2007. At the Cebu Summit Meeting, the "Joint Press Statement of the Seventh Summit Meeting among the People's Republic of China, Japan and the Republic of Korea" was announced. The leaders endorsed the 2005–2006 Progress Report of the Trilateral Cooperation among the People's Republic of China, Japan and the Republic of Korea and expressed satisfaction with the considerable progress made in various areas, especially in the five priority areas of economy and trade, ICT industry, environmental protection, human resources development and culture. At the Eighth Summit Meeting, which was held in Singapore on 20 November 2007, the leaders agreed to hold the Trilateral Summit Meeting independently from the ASEAN+3 Summit Meetings. The "Third Progress Report of the Trilateral Cooperation for 2007" and the "Action Plan for the Promotion of Tripartite Cooperation among the People's Republic of China, Japan and the Republic of Korea" were endorsed.[1]

Independent CJK summits

The First Independent Trilateral Summit took place in Fukuoka on 13 December 2008. Unlike the previous Trilateral Summit Meetings mentioned above, this Trilateral Summit was organized independently of the ASEAN+3 framework. The leaders decided to hold the Summit in the three countries on a regular basis and the "Joint Statement for Tripartite Partnership", the "Action Plan for Promoting Trilateral Cooperation among the People's Republic of China, Japan and the Republic of Korea", the "Trilateral Joint Announcement on Disaster Management Cooperation" and the "Joint Statement on the International Finance and Economy" were adopted at the Summit.

The Second Trilateral Summit was held in Beijing on 10 October 2009. On the occasion of the Tenth Anniversary of China-Japan-Korea Trilateral Cooperation, the leaders announced the "Joint Statement on the Tenth Anniversary of Trilateral Cooperation among the People's Republic of China, Japan and the Republic of Korea". The "Joint Statement on Sustainable Development among the

People's Republic of China, Japan and the Republic of Korea" was also adopted. In addition, the leaders agreed to launch the Official Tripartite Joint Study for a China-Japan-Korea FTA, and they also held a Trilateral Business Summit.

The Third Trilateral Summit took place in Jeju, Korea on 29–30 May 2010. At the Summit, the "Trilateral Cooperation VISION 2020", the "Memorandum on the Establishment of the Trilateral Cooperation Secretariat among the governments of the Republic of Korea, Japan and the People's Republic of China", the "Joint Statement on Strengthening Science and Innovation Cooperation among the Republic of Korea, Japan and the People's Republic of China", and the "Joint Statement on Standards Cooperation among the Republic of Korea, Japan and the People's Republic of China" were adopted.

At the Fourth Trilateral Summit, which was held in Tokyo on 21–22 May 2011, the "Summit Declaration", the "Cooperation on Disaster Management", the "Cooperation on Nuclear Safety", and the "Cooperation toward Sustainable Growth through Promotion of Renewable Energy and Energy Efficiency" were adopted. The leaders also agreed to conclude the Official Tripartite Joint Study for a China-Japan-Korea FTA within a year.

The Fifth Trilateral Summit took place in Beijing on 13 May 2012. At the Summit, along with the "Joint Declaration on the Enhancement of Trilateral Comprehensive Cooperative Partnership", the "Joint Statement of Cooperation on Sustainable Forest Management, Combating Desertification and Wildlife Conservation" and the "Joint Statement on Agricultural Cooperation" were adopted (MOFAT, Japan 2012). Furthermore, the leaders welcomed the conclusion and recommendations of the Joint Study for a FTA among the three countries. Recognizing that the establishment of a FTA among China, Japan and Korea would contribute to the economic growth and prosperity of the three countries, the heads of state endorsed the recommendations of the trade ministers that the trilateral FTA negotiation should be launched within the year. In order to achieve this aim, the heads of the three countries announced that they would immediately start preparations, including the development of domestic procedures and working-level consultations. In addition, the "Trilateral Investment Protection Agreement" was signed.

The Sixth Trilateral Summit was scheduled to be held in Korea in 2013. However, due to the deterioration of political relations among the three countries related to territorial disputes and historical issues, the Trilateral Summit did not take place in 2013–2014; it was held in Seoul on 1 November 2015. After the summit, the "Joint Declaration for Peace and Cooperation in Northeast Asia", together with the "Joint Statement on Environmental Cooperation", the "Joint Statement on Economy and Trade Cooperation", the "Joint Statement on Customs Cooperation on Trade Facilitation", the "Joint Statement on Agricultural Cooperation" and the "Joint Statement on Education Cooperation" were issued (MOFAT, Japan 2015).

According to the "Joint Declaration for Peace and Cooperation in Northeast Asia", acknowledging that steady progress has been made in trilateral cooperation in various areas despite the fluid political situation in the Northeast Asia region in recent years, the leaders shared the view that trilateral cooperation had been completely restored on the occasion of this Summit. It was, however, held almost three and half years after the Fifth Trilateral Summit held in May 2012. The leaders had come to the realization that respective bilateral ties among the three countries constitute an important foundation for trilateral cooperation, and that the deepening of trilateral cooperation, in turn, contributes to each bilateral relation and to peace, stability and prosperity of the Northeast Asia region. Thus, in the spirit of facing history squarely and advancing towards the future, the leaders agreed that the three countries should address related issues properly and work together to improve bilateral relations and strengthen trilateral cooperation.

Ministerial meetings

In addition to the Trilateral Summit Meetings, various Ministerial-level meetings took place among the three countries. Since December 2012, eighteen Trilateral Ministerial Meetings have been held under the independent Trilateral Summit umbrella, including the thirteen meetings related to economic issues. Among the thirteen economic issues-related Trilateral Ministerial Meetings, eight meetings take place every year in principle, including the Trilateral Foreign Ministers' Meeting, Trilateral Economic and Trade Ministers' Meeting, Environment Ministers' Meeting, Trilateral Finance Ministers' Meeting, Trilateral Culture Ministers' Meeting, Trilateral Agriculture Ministers' Meeting, Tripartite Health Ministers' Meeting and the Trilateral Policy Dialogue Meeting.

Four other economic-related Trilateral Ministerial Meetings are held every two years in rotation, including the Trilateral Ministerial Meeting on Science and Technology, Ministerial Conference on Transport and Logistics, Trilateral Tourism Ministers' Meeting and the Tripartite Customs Heads Meeting. In case of the Trilateral ICT Ministerial Meeting, despite the fact that the three countries have agreed to launch the meeting annually, only one meeting has taken place after the fourth Trilateral ICT Ministers' Meeting in 2006.

Most Trilateral Ministerial Meetings, except for the Trilateral Economic and Trade Ministers' Meeting, have supporting mechanisms such as the Director-General Meetings and the working-level meetings to implement and evaluate joint cooperation projects among the three countries. On the advent of the "Agreement of the Establishment of the Trilateral Cooperation Secretariat" signed and ratified by each of the three governments at the independent Trilateral Summit in 2010, the Trilateral Cooperation Secretariat (TCS) was officially inaugurated in September 2011. The main functions of the TCS include evaluating cooperative projects, submitting annual progress reports to the Trilateral Foreign Ministers' Meeting for approval, and providing administrative and technical support for the operation of the trilateral consultative mechanisms to solidify the cooperative ties among the three countries.

In order to better systematize the economic issues-related dialogue channels at the government level, the host country for the independent Trilateral Summit should also host the economic issues-related Ministerial Meetings. In addition, the three countries can adjust the schedule of the Trilateral Ministerial Meetings according to the independent Trilateral Summit. By strengthening this framework of government-level economic dialogue channels, the three countries can push forward the existing and potential cooperative projects. In addition, the Trilateral Cooperation Secretariat (TCS) needs to strengthen its functions related to conducting and compiling the annual progress report. This report is intended to provide a thorough and comprehensive evaluation of the cooperation initiatives which were endorsed by the leaders of the three countries during the independent Trilateral Summit.

CJK trilateral joint research

An important development that helped to lay the foundation for trilateral cooperation was the trilateral joint research on economic cooperation initiated by the three leaders at the Manila Summit Meeting. Based on this agreement, the Development Research Centre (DRC) of China, the National Institute for Research Advancement (NIRA)[2] of Japan and the Korea Institute for International Economic Policy (KIEP) began a joint research project in January 2001. The trilateral joint research was conducted from 2001 to 2012. Each year, the three institutions presented policy recommendations based on their joint research to the leaders of the three countries during the Trilateral Summit Meeting.

The first joint project began with joint research on trilateral trade cooperation and investment. This research took place over a period of two years, the first year of which was devoted to trade with a focus on trade facilitation issues and the second year was devoted to investment issues. The highlight of the trilateral joint research was the study on "Economic Effects of a Possible Free Trade Area among China, Japan and Korea",[3] which had been conducted since 2003. Although the joint research project was supposed to last about three years, it took seven years before it was finally concluded. This prolonged duration was a result of governments not being ready to upgrade it to an Official Tripartite Joint Study. At the same time, the governments did not want to stop the research for fear that it could weaken the momentum of the Trilateral FTA.

At the beginning of the trilateral joint research, government officials and business representatives participated only in the International Symposium where the results of each year's trilateral joint research were discussed. However, from 2006, business representatives of the three countries began to join the planning and mid-term workshops, and government officials also began to participate in those workshops as observers from 2007. Finally, in 2009, the three institutions recommended to the leaders of the three countries to upgrade the joint research on the CJK FTA to discussions among government officials of the three countries.

During the research project's seven years, the three institutions conducted four computable general equilibrium model simulations on macro-economic effects of the CJK FTA. Numerous studies were also conducted on sectoral implications for the major manufacturing industries such as automobile, chemical, electronic, general machinery, steel and textile, agriculture, fisheries, as well as major service sectors. Rules of origin and sensitive sectors were also examined. Furthermore, expectations of and obstacles to a CJK FTA were discussed and a possible road map for a CJK FTA was suggested.

Most importantly, based on the studies conducted during the period 2003–2009, the three institutions recommended that the leaders should upgrade the joint research on the CJK FTA by commencing discussions among officials of the three governments. The joint research teams reaffirmed the importance of a CJK FTA arguing that it would ensure a liberalized trade environment in the region and that the liberalized environment would greatly contribute to ensuring economic recovery in East Asia, as well as developing a strong source of macroeconomic final demand in the region.

The CJK FTA

Joint Study Committee for a China-Japan-Korea FTA

Based on the recommendation of the trilateral joint research, the leaders of China, Japan and Korea agreed to launch an Official Tripartite Joint Study for a CJK FTA at the second Trilateral Summit Meeting in Beijing in October 2009. Accordingly, the first Joint Study Committee (JSC) for a CJK FTA took place in Seoul in May 2010, and the Joint Study was concluded at the seventh meeting, which was held in Pyeongchang, Korea in December 2011.[4] The JSC examined the coverage of the possible CJK FTA without prejudice to the future positions of the three countries in possible trilateral FTA negotiations. A possible trilateral FTA was expected to address trade in goods, trade in services, investment and other issues that may include, but not be limited to, technical barriers to trade, sanitary and phytosanitary measures, intellectual property rights, transparency, competition policy, dispute settlement mechanism, industrial cooperation, consumer safety, e-commerce, energy and mineral resources, fisheries, food, government procurement and the environment.[5]

The JSC also agreed on the four guiding principles which would be applied to the CJK FTA negotiations: first, the CJK FTA should pursue a comprehensive and high-level FTA; second, the CJK FTA should be consistent with WTO rules; third, the CJK FTA should strive for balanced results and achieve a win-win-win situation on the basis of reciprocity and mutual benefit; and fourth, the negotiations should be conducted in a constructive and positive manner, with due consideration to the sensitive sectors in each country. The JSC also added that it shared the view that strong political will would be needed during the entire process for a CJK FTA. The outcome of the Joint Study was reported to the Economic and Trade Ministers' Meeting and the Fifth Trilateral Summit Meeting, which took place in Beijing in May 2012. The leaders welcomed the conclusion and recommendations of the Joint Study for a CJK FTA and endorsed the recommendations from the trade ministers that the trilateral FTA negotiation should be launched in 2012. The leaders added that to achieve this end, the three countries should immediately start preparations including developing domestic procedures and working-level consultations.[6] The trade ministers of the three countries met in Phnom Penh, Cambodia, on 20 November 2012 on the occasion of the twenty-first ASEAN summit and related summits and announced the launch of the CJK FTA negotiations. The Ministers further decided that the first round of the trilateral FTA negotiations would be held in early 2013.

Current status of CJK FTA negotiations

The first official negotiations on a CJK FTA were held in Seoul from 26–28 March 2013 following a preparatory meeting held in Tokyo the previous month. The second round of negotiations were held in Shanghai from 30 July-2 August 2013 and was conducted, as the first meeting, at the deputy minister level. This round discussed trade in goods, trade in services, custom procedures, competition policies and intellectual property. Since March 2018, thirteen rounds of FTA negotiations and a number of working-level meetings have been held. The last round of negotiations was held in Seoul, Korea between 22 and 23 March 2018 where trade in goods, trade in services and investment were the key issues under discussion. Most of the thirteen rounds of FTA negotiations have been held at the deputy minister's level and have generally focused on trade in goods, trade in services and investment. The fourteenth round of negotiations is scheduled to be held in China. Details of negotiations to date are provided in Table 4.1 below (see also China FTA Net 2017; MFAJ 2017). In addition to these negotiations a trilateral investment agreement was signed by all three nations in 2014 (Tiezzi 2014).

In the five years since the launch of CJK FTA negotiations, these negotiations have not produced tangible results, although some limited progress has been made. The slow progress of the CJK FTA negotiations and their limited results can be explained primarily by two factors: the lack of leadership and the weakened momentum towards a CJK FTA. In the case of all three countries this delay has been due to a concentration on other ongoing FTA negotiations. China and Korea were more focused on the China-Korea FTA negotiations than the CJK FTA negotiations during the period of their bilateral FTA negotiations. Likewise, Japan was focused primarily on the TPP negotiations; both before and after the US withdrawal.

Perhaps of more importance in this respect has been the significant deterioration of Sino-Japanese relations as well as the Japanese-Korean relations since the launch of the CJK FTA negotiation. Although the Trilateral Summit was supposed to be held annually, the Sixth Trilateral Summit took place in November 2015, almost three and half years after the Fifth Trilateral Summit held in May 2012. Under these circumstances, the negotiators of the three countries appear to have attempted to acquire more favourable positions for their countries before entering into real negotiations. Given that the China-Korea FTA was concluded and is in effect, and the TPP negotiations have been concluded and have been signed off (excluding the US), although not in effect at this stage, the prospects for CJK FTA negotiations will depend largely on the changes in political relations among the three countries. As mentioned above, the leaders of the three countries were instrumental in the CJK FTA since its preparation period,

Table 4.1 FTA negotiations – China, Japan and South Korea

Round	*Date*	*Location*	*Level*	*Listed Discussion Areas*
1a	20–21 Feb 2013	Tokyo	Working-level officials	Preparatory meeting for first round of negotiations
1b	26–28 March 2013	Seoul	Deputy Minister	Scope and method of negotiations
1c	3–4 June 2013	Tokyo	Working-level officials	Preparatory meeting for second round of negotiations
2	30 July-2 Aug 2013	Shanghai	Deputy Minister	Trade in goods, trade in services, custom procedures, competition policies, intellectual property
3a	22–23 Oct 2013	Seoul	Working-level officials	Preparatory meeting for third round of negotiations
3b	26–29 Nov 2013	Tokyo	Deputy Minister	Trade in goods, trade in services, competition policies, intellectual property
4	4–7 March 2014	Tokyo	Deputy Minister	Trade in goods, trade in services, competition policies, intellectual property
5a	17–18 June 2014	Tokyo	Working-level officials	Intersessional meeting for the negotiations on FTA
5b	1–5 Sept 2014	Beijing	Deputy Minister	Trade in goods, trade in services, investment, competition policies, intellectual property
6	16–17 Jan 2015	Tokyo	Deputy Minister	Trade in goods, trade in services, investment
7a	13–17 April 2015	Seoul	Deputy Director-General	Trade in goods, trade in services, investment, competition policies, intellectual property
7b	12–13 May 2015	Seoul	Deputy Minister	Trade in goods, trade in services, investment
8a	20–24 July 2015	Beijing	Deputy Director-General	Trade in goods, trade in services, investment, competition policies, intellectual property
8b	24–25 Sept 2015	Beijing	Deputy Minister	Trade in goods, trade in services, investment
9	18–19 Jan 2016	Tokyo	Deputy Minister	Trade in goods, trade in services, investment
10	4–9 April 2016	Seoul	Deputy Director-General	Trade in goods, trade in services, investment, competition policies, intellectual property
11	9–11 Jan 2017	Beijing	Deputy Minister	Trade in goods, trade in services, investment
12	10–13 April 2017	Tokyo	Deputy Minister	Trade in goods, trade in services, investment
13	22–23 March 2018	Seoul	Deputy Minister	Trade in goods, trade in services, investment

Source: Ministry of Foreign Affairs of Japan (2018) (www.mofa.go.jp/policy/economoc/fta/index.html) (accessed on 22 March 2018).

and the negotiations started after the agreement reached at the Fifth Trilateral Summit Meeting in Beijing.

Finally, the Trilateral Summit process was resumed, and at the Sixth Trilateral Summit, the leaders of the three countries reaffirmed that the Trilateral Summit is to be held on a regular basis in the three countries, as specified in the 2008 Joint Statement for Tripartite Partnership. Furthermore, reiterating their commitment to the Trilateral Cooperation VISION 2020 to work towards further economic integration in the long-term, including the establishment of a common market in the region, the leaders reconfirmed that they would make further efforts towards the acceleration of the trilateral FTA negotiations to realize a comprehensive, high-level and mutually beneficial FTA.[7] However, as far as the CJK FTA negotiations are concerned, two years after the Sixth Trilateral Summit, it still appears to be too early to ascertain any positive spill over effects.

Conclusion

In order to realize the era of East Asia, the region has to maintain its economic growth, enlarge internal markets and create a stable international political and security environment. To satisfy all these conditions, a region-wide FTA in East Asia is needed. Given the many FTAs among East Asian countries, including ASEAN+1 FTAs, the remaining missing links are among the three Northeast Asian countries. Thus, in order to move forward on a region-wide FTA in East Asia, the formation of a FTA or FTAs between China, Japan and Korea is required. On the other hand, the vision of realizing the East Asia era could be used as an additional stimulus to push forward the formation of a region-wide FTA in East Asia and a CJK FTA. For this to occur, China, Japan and Korea must strive to form a region-wide FTA in the mid and long term, and in the short term, should focus on the formation of a CJK FTA. By choosing a trilateral FTA (over bilateral FTAs), the three countries could also demonstrate their willingness to assume leadership in improving relations in Northeast Asia.

Notes

1 The Ninth, Tenth and Eleventh Trilateral Summit Meetings were held in Pattaya Thailand on 11 April 2009, in Hanoi on 29 October 2010, and Bali on 19 November 2011, respectively.
2 Since 2009, the Institute of Developing Economies (IDE-JETRO) is the representative institution for Japan.
3 The Japanese government was initially reluctant to accept the choice of the CJK FTA topic of "Economic Effects from a Possible FTA between China, Japan and Korea."
4 The other meetings were held in Tokyo (second), Weihai, China (third), Jeju, Korea (fourth), Kitakyushu, Japan (fifth) and Changchun, China (sixth).
5 Joint Study Report for a FTA between China, Japan and Korea, 16 December 2011.
6 Joint Declaration on the Enhancement of Trilateral Comprehensive Cooperative Partnership, the Fifth Trilateral Summit (Beijing, 13 May 2012).
7 Joint Declaration for Peace and Cooperation in Northeast Asia, the Sixth Trilateral Summit (Seoul, 1 November 2015).

5 The political economy of economic clustering in Northeast Asia

Introduction

As discussed in Chapter 4, during the annual China-Japan-South Korea (CJK) summit, held on 13 May 2012 in Beijing, leaders of CJK stated their intention to begin negotiations on a trilateral free trade agreement. Despite the territorial conflict over many years among CJK countries, the launch of the Free Trade Agreement (FTA) negotiations among these countries was announced at the CJK Economic and Trade Ministers' Meeting held in Phnom Penh, Cambodia, on 20 November 2012. Negotiations between the three countries focusing on strategies to achieve a larger and more comprehensive economic clustering in the region took over a decade to reach this stage. The decision of CJK to work towards some form of economic cluster represents the growing economic dependency and integration of these economies where competition is giving way to more complementary activities and a realization that much is to be gained by each country cooperating in trade, investment and industry.

While Northeast Asian economic cooperation has only been sporadically achieved and its future remains uncertain, primarily due to the historical, cultural, political and economic characteristics of the region, the new millenium has brought about a greater desire between China, Japan and Korea for increased economic integration, regional trade and investment relations, financial and environmental cooperation, science and technology exchange and industrial cooperation. The three countries have a population of more than 1.5 billion (21 per cent of the world's population), and more than US $150 trillion of GDP, which represented 20 per cent of the world's total trade and foreign direct investment as of 2015.[1] CJK's trade volume comprises over 18 per cent of the world trade volume. Compared to the trade volume of other economic blocs such as the EU (32 per cent), NAFTA (16 per cent) and ASEAN (7 per cent), CJK represents a significant share of global trade. China has been the largest trading partner of Japan and Korea for some years. Japan is the fourth largest and Korea the sixth largest trading partner of China, and the trilateral trade volume increased from US $130 billion in 1999 to $690 billion in 2011. Although the recent (2015) intra-regional trade ratio of CJK (19 per cent) is lower than that of other major economic blocs such as ASEAN (24 per cent), NAFTA (42 per cent) and the EU

(65 per cent) (Trilateral Cooperation Secretariat 2017), these three countries are important economic and trade partners. Moreover, current trilateral cooperation projects such as the CJK FTA will further expand this level of intra-regional trade.

Despite the socio-economic and political significance of the new vision for each of these countries, many academics and policy makers doubt the feasibility of this new regional economic architecture in Northeast Asia because of the political, historical and cultural differences among the CJK members. Many questions remain unanswered, including how well a CJK FTA would work, whether it could continue to work in the future, which country among CJK benefits most from this new form of economic integration, how changes of leadership in CJK will influence the progress of the CJK FTA, and whether China's progressive approach to the new Asian regionalism will reduce the influence of the US's preferred Asian regional architecture, or whether less influence from the US, such as moving away from the Trans-Pacific Strategic Partnership Agreement (TPP), would enhance China's leadership position in the region and push Japan and Korea towards China for economic integration. This chapter addresses these questions and begins with a discussion of the rationale and structure of this potential Northeast Asia FTA. The chapter then examines critical issues and challenges (socio-economic and geo-political) for a CJK FTA.

Northeast Asian regionalism

As discussed in previous chapters, the push towards economic integration in Northeast Asia has strengthened in recent years. This drive has taken various forms but has been led most recently by the CJK FTA negotiations. Thirteen rounds of negotiations have taken place over the past five years (see Table 4.1) although there are few tangible results. This slow rate of progress is due to the formable barriers to the development of a smooth regional integration arrangement. These barriers are generally due to certain fundamental differences in political systems, current territorial and historical disputes and a lack of community consciousness (Choi 2013: 105). On the other hand, certain important economic needs require addressing among the three countries, including closer economic links with geographic and psychic (cultural) proximity, complementary endowments of production factors and increasing economic interdependence.

Developments towards deepening CJK economic ties and integration are underpinned by the outbreak of the 1997 Asian financial crisis, the intensification of economic integration of the EU and NAFTA (although not without difficulties), China's WTO accession in 2001 and its increasing global economic power and the global financial and the European fiscal crises. These events brought about a consensus among the key policy makers of CJK that they needed to reduce their dependence on exports outside the region (to the US and the EU in particular) and base their economic growth more firmly on domestic or regional demand in order to stabilize the global as well as the regional economy. The governments of CJK declared that there was much to be gained from the CJK FTA which would eliminate both tariff and non-tariff barriers and ultimately lead to a common market. The most fundamental and obvious rationale behind this claim are the benefits from the deepening of regional economic interdependence; these include geographic and psychic (cultural) proximity, complementary endowments of production factors, and increasing economic ties. Other economic benefits from the institutional agreements are (a) increased market access to goods, services, skills and technology, (b) increased market size to permit specialization and realization of economies of scale, (c) the facilitation of foreign direct investment (FDI) activities and technology transfer of multinational corporations (MNCs) and (d) the simplification of tariff schedules, rules and standards. However, there are a number of non-market factors such as regional, geo-political and environmental factors (i.e. security, international relations, domestic politics and the rise of the Chinese economy), or in Solis and Katada's (2007) words, 'leverage motives', that need to be considered in any analysis of the 'cross regionalism' moves in Northeast Asia since the 1997 Asian financial crisis.

China

China, Japan and Korea are now increasingly the leading players in the development of FTAs and the integration of economies. Since December 2017, China has concluded fourteen FTAs; namely, with Hong Kong, Macao, New Zealand, ASEAN, Chile, Singapore, Peru, Pakistan, Costa Rica, Switzerland, Iceland, Maldives, Georgia and Australia (see Table 5.1 for further details). China is also currently negotiating FTAs with the GCC (Gulf Cooperation Council), the SACU

Table 5.1 China's FTAs by status and geographical orientation (as of September 2017)

	Intra East Asia FTA	*Extra East Asia FTA*
Implemented	Hong Kong (CEPA) Macau (CEPA) Taipei (ECFA) Korea ASEAN+6	Asia-Pacific Trade Agreement (APTA) Chile Pakistan Australia Costa Rica Peru Thailand Singapore Georgia Iceland
Under negotiation		South African Customs Union Gulf Cooperation Council Maldives Sri Lanka
Proposed/Under consultation and study	ASEAN+3 China-Japan-Korea	Shanghai Cooperation Organization India Norway

Source: Asia Regional Integration Centre (2017) https://aric.adb.org/fta-country) (accessed on 13 December 2017).

(Southern African Customs Union), Norway, CJK, Singapore, Mauritius, Sri Lanka, Japan and RCEP (China FTA Network 2017). China's FTA objectives and strategies are based on the following priorities (China FTA Network 2017):[2]

- the completion of Chinese (overseas) economic zone and the economic dominance in the Asian region
- the stability in the region (e.g. Pakistan and ASEAN)
- the acquiring energy for its economic growth (Chile and GCC)
- the political and economic stability in Northeast Asia (Japan and Korea)
- the expansion and diversification of markets (e.g. Australia, New Zealand and Switzerland)
- the final stage of the unification of China (Hong Kong, Macao and Taiwan).

From a China perspective, the process of negotiation for a CJK FTA has not been smooth and delays have occurred from time to time in the past decade, due to the geo-political tensions with Japan and South Korea. For example, due to the tension between China and Japan rooted in the island dispute of Diaoyu/Senkaku, particularly since 2012, when the Japanese government nationalized this island, the bilateral relationship between the two countries has been deteriorating until recent months when the top leaders of both countries indicated their willingness to improve the relationship. The relationship with South Korea has been troubled, starting with the response of the US and South Korea to North Korea's nuclear/missile testing with the deployment of the THAAD (Terminal High Altitude Area Defence) missile system. The Chinese viewed this action as an excuse for using the North Korean problem to build the capability to monitor Chinese military movement through the THAAD system (Padden 2017). Consequently, the political relationship between former President Park's regime and the Chinese leadership under President Xi was damaged. The economic relationship was also affected by the Chinese government's scrutiny of South Korean businesses operating in China as well as blocking Chinese tourists visiting South Korea (Padden 2017).

Since the second half of 2017, China's relationships with both Japan and South Korea have been improving. A much warmer relationship between China and Japan started with top party officials of the Japanese LDP visiting China with a personal letter from Prime Minister Abe to President Xi indicating a desire to repair the relationship. Subsequently, two important top leadership meetings, including President Xi's meeting with Prime Minister Abe in Hanoi during the APEC Summit and Premier Li's meeting with Prime Minister Abe in Manila during the East Asia Summit. Prime Minister Abe openly supported the Chinese initiative of 'One Belt and One Road', and indicated that Japan would fully engaged with this initiative, in particular by developing cooperative projects with China in other countries (Chen and Wang 2017).

China's relationship with South Korea has also improved since President Moon assumed power. Following the deployment of four THAAD carrying trucks, President Moon stopped further deployment. After his visit to China and meeting with President Xi (Gao 2017), the South Korean government stressed that the deployment of THAAD system was aimed at protecting South Korea from an attack from the North and there was no intention to target any Chinese military site. The South Korean government also promised China that it would monitor the use of the THAAD system and ensure the deployment would not exceed the geographical limit beyond the North Korean territory. Since then, the relationship has developed with improved political trust and economic ties. In addition, the South Korean government has been very supportive of the Chinese initiative of 'One Belt and One Road' and is one of the funding members of the Chinese led 'Asian Infrastructure and Investment Bank' (AIIB), which provides financial support to realize the goals of the 'One Belt and One Road' initiative (Lee 2016).

Political and strategic tensions have not only damaged the relationships among the three countries from time to time, but also delayed the momentum of achieving the common goal of establishing a CJK FTA. There are several issues that are important to China specifically and the Chinese have attempted to drive negotiations in line with these fundamental issues. In addition, an eventual agreement has the potential to also generate a number of economic and political win-win outcomes for China.

The Chinese leadership clearly sees the CJK FTA as a positive initiative for political and economic integration in the Northeast Asian region. Commenting on the CJK FTA, President Xi stated, "The parties should cherish the principles of openness, inclusiveness and transparency and, in particular, demonstrate flexibility for economies at different development stages, to offer more options for integration" (Cited in Yoshimatsu 2015: 114). Based on these principles, the Chinese government sees the three countries' engagement with this FTA to include geographic and psychic (cultural) proximity, complementary endowments of production factors and increasing economic ties. The economic benefits of institutional agreements include (a) increased market access to goods, services, skills and technology, (b) increased market size to permit specialization and realization of economies of scale, (c) facilitated FDI activities and technology transfer of MNCs and (d permit simplification of tariff schedules, rules and standards (Kawai and Wignaraja 2010a: 20). From China's perspective, a CJK FTA would also give a foothold for further integration in Asia, free up production supply chains (concentration on manufacturing), offer enhanced economic security for the new Chinese leadership, enable China to expand and internationalize its currency (RMB) and so reduce its reliance on the US dollar, see higher quality products exported to China and offer improved market opportunities for both state-owned enterprises (SOEs) and private companies. These strong political and economic pressures and expectations have motivated China to push for the realization of the CJK FTA.

Another important reason for the Chinese government supporting the CJK FTA initiative are the geo-political tensions with the US. The US-led TPP initiative gradually developed momentum among twelve Asia-Pacific countries, albeit without the involvement of China. The Chinese thus seek to develop an alternative free trade forum where they can exert some influence. Hence, China believes an ASEAN-led RCEP would be an appropriate way to move forward in terms of regional economic integration and the formation of the CJK FTA could be a useful platform for further engagement between the two trading blocks of Northeast and Southeast Asian regions, without the US influence (Lee, Benson and Zhu 2015: 38). Given the US withdrawal from the TPP in 2017, the major Asian economies are now seeking to develop a more workable free trade arrangement within the region, including negotiating a CJK FTA, and then the subsequent establishment of the RCEP.

So far, there have been several key disagreements between China and the other two parties during the negotiation process for a CJK FTA. In the early years of negotiations, China's position on an investment treaty was rather straight forward; namely, the three countries should first form a trilateral investment treaty. The investment chapter of a CJK FTA should then simply follow what was agreed in the trilateral investment treaty. However, Japan and Korea believe that it is pointless to sign a FTA unless the investment chapter shows a significant improvement; investment scope and coverage, as well as the level of ambition, should be very different from the trilateral investment treaty (Hamanaka 2017: 135).

Another area of disagreement is on free trade-related intellectual property in the context of the CJK FTA negotiations. A number of major factors influence China's stance on intellectual property; namely, its stage of economic development, innovation capacity and level of intellectual property enforcement (Zhang 2016). Though China is expressly against the Trade-Related Aspects of Intellectual Property Rights (TRIPS)-Plus standards for intellectual property enforcement, its attitude towards intellectual property issues in FTA negotiations is fairly flexible. With intellectual property becoming increasingly important for China's innovation-driven economy and with higher standards of intellectual property enforcement being incorporated into other FTAs such as the TPP, China's stance on intellectual property in future FTA negotiations will eventually change (Zhang 2016).

In 2017, two rounds of negotiations – the eleventh and twelfth rounds – were held in Beijing in January and Tokyo in April respectively. The twelfth round of negotiations began on 10 April 2017 in Tokyo. The three parties held working group meetings on trade in services, telecommunications, financial services, natural persons, investment, competition policy, intellectual property rights and e-commerce and conducted a comprehensive and detailed policy exchange on management measures regarding trade in services (China FTA Network 2017). The most recent round of negotiations, namely the thirteenth round, was held in Seoul on 22 and 23 March 2018. The delegates examined progress on key issues, such as product negotiation guidelines, service liberalization methods and investment reservation negotiations. They also discussed the road map for accelerating negotiations and exchanged information about policies and institutions in the fields of services, finance and telecommunications (Kim and Hahm 2018).

China's position in the recent rounds of negotiations has become more open and flexible given that the current geo-political and economic environments require China to play a greater leadership role (e.g. the influence of the Trump administration's 'America First' approach). The Chinese official position is that as

> China has become the centre of East Asian economy, we should be more open and tolerant to different ideas and push forward the realization of CJK FTA. A high-quality FTA can be formed by including investment treaty, government purchase, intellectual property protection, competition policy, e-commerce, labour protection issues and environmental protection.
>
> (Zhang 2017)

China's FTA strategy is concisely summarized by one Chinese official who claimed,

> A step-by-step manner is adopted, including coordinating the current FTA treaties with consistent approach, lifting the standards through new bilateral and multilateral FTA negotiations, cooperating the development of economic corridor and special economic zones in third country and connecting the dots of FTAs and Economic Zones globally. By doing so, China can promote the establishment of open global economy which is one of the central goals of the 19th CCP Congress.
>
> (Zhang 2017)

Japan

Similarly to China and South Korea, Japan has been active in securing FTAs over the last decade or so. As of October 2017, Japan had fifteen Free Trade Agreements (FTAs – some are referred to as Economic Partnership Agreements[3] or EPAs); namely those with Singapore, Mexico, Malaysia, Chile, Thailand, Indonesia, Brunei, ASEAN, the Philippines, Switzerland, Vietnam, India, Peru, Australia and Mongolia. In addition, the TPP has been signed (and the subsequent CPTTP) but is not in effect. Japan is also active in pursuing further agreements and currently has eight FTAs/EPAs under negotiation, including those with Canada, Columbia, the EU, the GCC, South Korea, Turkey, CJK and the RGEP. In addition, five IIAs (International Investment Agreements) have been signed and are 'in force' with Iran, Kazakhstan, Oman, Ukraine and Uruguay. Details are provided in Table 5.2.

The South Korea FTA negotiations have been running the longest, having commenced in 2003, although they were suspended in 2004 (MOFAT, Korea 2011) and have proven difficult to restart due to the underlying political tensions. Recently, meaningful discussions have taken place to resume these bilateral FTA negotiations. One of the most distinctive developments in recent years in Japan's EPA negotiations are the recently (December 2017) concluded EPA negotiations with the EU. It is expected that the deal will be signed, ratified and implemented in 2019. This will have significant implications for the rest of East Asia and beyond. This new deal will forge an economic zone of 600 million people with a value of 30 per cent of the global gross domestic product.[4]

Table 5.2 Japan's FTAs (as of December 2017)

Type[1]	*Country*	*Status*	*Date*
Trade Agreements			
EPA	Canada	Negotiations Launched	26–11–2012
EPA	Columbia	Negotiations Launched	17–12–2012
EPA	European Union[2]	Negotiations Launched	15–04–2013
FTA	Gulf Cooperation Council[3]	Negotiations Launched	21–09–2006
FTA	South Korea	Negotiations Launched	22–12–2003
EPA	Turkey	Negotiations Launched	02–12–2014
FTA	China-Japan-Korea[4]	Negotiations Launched	26–03–2013
FTA	Regional Comprehensive Economic Partnership (RGEP)[5]	Negotiations Launched	09–05–2013
FTA	Trans-Pacific Partnership (TPP)[6]	Signed but not In Effect	04–02–2016
FTA	Association of South East Asian Nations (ASEAN)[7]	Signed and In Effect	01–12–2008
EPA	Australia	Signed and In Effect	15–01–2015
FTA	Brunei	Signed and In Effect	31–07–2008
EPA	Chile	Signed and In Effect	03–09–2007
CEPA	India	Signed and In Effect	01–08–2011
EPA	Indonesia	Signed and In Effect	01–07–2008
EPA	Malaysia	Signed and In Effect	13–07–2006
EPA	Mexico	Signed and In Effect	01–04–2005
EPA	Mongolia	Signed and In Effect	07–06–2016
FTA	Peru	Signed and In Effect	01–03–2012
EPA	Philippines	Signed and In Effect	11–12–2008
EANAP	Singapore	Signed and In Effect	30–11–2002
EPA	Switzerland	Signed and In Effect	01–09–2009
EPA	Thailand	Signed and In Effect	01–11–2007
EPA	Vietnam	Signed and In Effect	01–10–2009
Investment Agreements			
IIA	Iran	Signed and In Force	05–02–2016
IIA	Kazakhstan	Signed and In Force	23–10–2014
IIA	Oman	Signed and In Force	19–06–2015
IIA	Ukraine	Signed and In Force	05–02–2015
IIA	Uruguay	Signed and In Force	27–01–2015

Source: Asia Regional Integration Centre (2017) (https://aric.adb.org/fta-country); Ministry of Economy Trade and Industry (Japan) press releases (www.meti.go.jp/english/policy/external_economy/trade/FTA_EPA/index.html).

Notes:

1 Economic Partnership Agreement (EPA), Free Trade Agreement (FTA), Comprehensive Economic Partnership Agreement (CEPA), Economic Agreement for a New-Age Partnership (EANAP), International Investment Agreement (IIA).

2 Austria, Belgium, Bulgaria, Cyprus, Czech Republic, Denmark, Estonia, Finland, France, Germany, Greece, Hungary, Ireland, Italy, Latvia, Lithuania, Luxembourg, Malta, Netherlands, Poland, Portugal, Romania, Slovakia, Slovenia, Spain, Sweden, United Kingdom.

3 Bahrain, Kuwait, Oman, Qatar, Saudi Arabia, United Arab Emirates.

4 China, Japan and South Korea.

5 Australia, Cambodia, India, Laos, Myanmar, Philippines, Thailand, Brunei, China, Indonesia, South Korea, Malaysia, New Zealand, Singapore, Vietnam.

6 Australia, Chile, Peru, United States, Brunei, New Zealand, Singapore, Vietnam, Malaysia, Canada, Mexico. The United States withdrew on 23 January 2017; this agreement has been reduced somewhat and has become the CPTTP.

7 Brunei, Cambodia, Indonesia, Laos, Malaysia, Myanmar, Philippines, Singapore, Thailand, Vietnam.

One significant development in 2017 was the withdrawal of the US from the TPP. This decision was made by the Trump administration in January 2017. Despite this setback, the remaining eleven countries (see Table 5.2) have signed a revised pact following talks in Tokyo, now called the Comprehensive and Progressive Agreement for Trans-Pacific Partnership (CPTPP). The CPTPP incorporates much of the original TPP but with an endorsed list of twenty suspended provisions (The Edge Financial Daily 26 January 2018: 17). These suspended provisions covering "trade facilitation, investment, services, public procurement, intellectual property rights, the environment and transparency" (Straits Times 23 January 2018), were primarily included as a condition of US participation and agreement. It remains to be seen if the US reverses its stance and whether the suspended items will be re-instated.

Whilst the CPTTP has been welcomed by the remaining countries, it is significantly narrower in scope than the TPP, with the remaining countries having only about 35 per cent of the GDP of the original twelve countries (Straits Times 23 January 2018). The withdrawal of the US from the TPP will be felt most strongly by Japan given its desire to open up further markets for its manufacturing goods and the threats from the Trump Administration to look closely at what it considers unfair trade agreements, including those with Japan. In contrast Japan has played a pivotal role in the CPTTP and in doing so has demonstrated some independence from the US despite its reliance on the US defence arrangements. In large part the reason for this action by Japan is to counter the growing influence of China by "seeking to defend the rules-based economic order in the Asia-Pacific region" (Reynolds and Tweed 2018: 16).

Given this recent flurry of FTA activity, what would a CJK FTA offer Japan? Clearly key benefits would include significant market opportunities for many types of Japanese companies, an increased market for capital goods and increased investment opportunities. Equally importantly, the realization of such a FTA would incorporate Japan into the region's economic power structure and the increased competitiveness would benefit the region and beyond. Japan views the CJK FTA as a vehicle to achieve a number of commercial objectives including Japan's further trade expansion to China and market access, Japan's incorporation of high-standard elements into the CJK FTA and expansion of Japanese companies' production networks and supply chains in East Asia (Yoshimatsu 2015: 114).

Such a FTA is subject to a range of competing interests in Japan. The country's Ministry of Economy, Trade and Industry (METI) claims that three broad principles underpin its support for FTAs/EPAs – namely, mutual prosperity, stable supply of resources and energy and access to large markets (METI 2007: 2). These principles take into account the growth and dynamism in Asia, the need to develop production networks of Asian companies, the need to invest in countries rich in resources so as to maintain supply and the need to develop competitive access to larger markets such as the US and the EU (METI 2007). In addition, METI supports a shift from bilateral agreements to region-wide economic integration such as the signing of ASEAN-Japan Comprehensive Economic Partnership Agreement (METI 2007: 5). Such a multi-layered style of integration has the potential to lead to trade and investment liberalization and the narrowing of the economic gap in the region (METI 2007: 12). Given these basic principles which appear to have strong government support for FTAs (and by extension a CJK FTA), why has the CJK FTA proven to be so elusive?

In attempting to answer this question, Greenberg (2015) suggests four possible reasons from a Japanese perspective for the lack of progress in reaching agreement: low economic priority, negative effect on agriculture, Korea's relative gains in the Chinese market and historical and political animosities. Each of these explanations has some merit, although with the conclusion of the CPTTP various government agencies and business positions may change. It is important to recognize that, when considering the relative merits of these four propositions, public opinion may not always align with political or business reality. Clearly, however, governments and business must be aware of such sentiments and not distance themselves from their constituencies.

Is a CJK FTA indeed an economic priority for Japan? Greenberg (2015: 41–50) suggests that the low priority given by Japan to this FTA has been a key factor in impeding progress of this trilateral arrangement. Keidanren, the major peak employer body, was generally supportive and for a short period placed a high priority on the CJK (2010–2011) through arrangements such as an ASEAN+3 agreement. By 2012, however, support had shifted to the TPP. The government adopted a similar stance to Keidanren through its agencies (METI and Japanese External Trade Organization (JETRO)). The general feeling was that the TPP offered better prospects for tariff reduction and going beyond the WTO requirements (Greenberg 2015: 49). In the current CPTTP environment (TPP minus the US) such an explanation will have less explanatory power.

The second explanation is that the Japanese agricultural sector may not see such a CJK FTA as being in their best economic interest. Whilst industry insiders may foresee a negative impact on Japanese agriculture, such as market loss and the corresponding income loss, as well as loss of intellectual property protection (DRC/NIRA/KIEP 2004: 6), both the large and politically influential Japanese Agricultural Cooperative (JA-Zenchu) and the Ministry of Agriculture, Forestry and Fisheries (MAFF) have been generally supportive of a CJK FTA (Greenberg 2015: 50). This support has been premised on serious exemptions being accorded to agriculture in any final agreement. JA-Zenchu and MAFF also view a CJK FTA as a 'hedge against the TPP' and currently in the best interests of agriculture (Greenberg 2015: 50). The third explanation relates to whether Japan is concerned with the potentially relative gains of Korea in the Chinese domestic market. In general, Keidanren, METI and JETRO (as well as Japanese MNCs) do not see Korea as a competitive threat to Japan. In non-agricultural sectors, Japanese tariffs are low, leading to a competitive domestic market which places them in a good position for the Chinese and Korean markets (DRC/NIRA/KIEP 2011: 14). The general feeling is that the greatest threat to Japanese firms in China is not Korean competitors but rather the increase in Chinese domestic competition and the slowdown in the Chinese economy (Greenberg 2015: 49). Clearly then these two explanations do not go far in explaining, from a Japanese perspective, the lack of progress towards a CJK FTA.

The final explanation relates to the impact of history and the present political environment. Past conflicts between Japan, and China and Korea have left a legacy of mistrust between the CJK partners, and contested claims on islands and sea boundaries have continued to surface from time to time. The election of nationalist leaders in all three countries, coupled with strong nationalistic tendencies, also feed into this potential explanation. Whilst such factors affect Japanese sentiment (and public sentiment in China and Korea), business has and continues to overcome such obstacles when they have arisen. As Greenberg (2015: 62) concluded, Keidanren and Japanese multinational companies have been able to see past such animosities and maintain business and government relationships, even during periods of heightened tension. In recent years this has been a more difficult task for their relationships in Korea, although more recently this bilateral relationship has been improving. Overall, this factor has not been a major impediment to a CJK FTA moving forward.

For Japan, the pursuit of FTAs is important, although it is not clear whether a bilateral agreement or a more ambitious FTA, such as an agreement with China and Korea, is preferred. The CJK FTA faces a number of difficulties and also has a number of advantages. In general, the CJK FTA (although not limited to a FTA) suffers from "competing historical narratives, territorial disputes and divergent strategic interests" (Sakaki and Wacker 2017: 33). The geopolitics of this region, coupled with the competition between China and the US, where the US has strong links with both Japan and Korea, will make such an agreement difficult to reach. Under Prime Minister Abe, Japan has sought wider security arrangements and this, coupled with the issue of North Korea, has fed into a higher level of mistrust between China and Japan. Higher levels of mistrust create political tensions which, in turn, lead to 'political' interventions in FTA negotiations.

Notwithstanding the difficulties outlined above, a CJK FTA has a number of advantages for Japan. This is more the case now, as over the past decade or two Japan has lost some of its considerable economic pre-eminence. Trade links between the CJK members are close (Sakaki and Wacker 2017: 5) and the Japanese government must build on these relationships, resisting the temptation to bring nationalistic sentiments into the negotiations. If Japan wishes to play a pivotal role in the region it will need to integrate more closely into the region's economic structures and gain the complementary benefits a CJK FTA will provide. As the Joint Study Report concluded, a CJK FTA

> would serve as an important vehicle that would strengthen existing relations of the three countries not only by expanding trilateral and bilateral trade and investment but also by providing a comprehensive and institutional framework in which a wide range of trilateral cooperation would evolve.
>
> (DRC/NIRA/KIEP 2011: 146)

Korea

The main advantage to Korea of a CJK FTA is that China's eagerness in seeking a FTA with Korea provides an opportunity to seek strong economic returns and hence enhance its position in CJK. Such an agreement will also have a critical strategic value in providing enhanced leverage over North Korea. In its relations with China, the CJK FTA and a bilateral FTA with China represents for Korea a heavily focused political-security and economy-driven model.

Since the 1997 Asian financial crisis, Korea has been determined to become a regional FTA hub nation in an effort to overcome its relatively small domestic market and participate actively in a rapidly regionalized world. In fact, until its first FTA with Chile in 2004, Korea had not negotiated any bilateral trade agreement, nor did it have a clear strategy for FTAs with foreign countries. The 1997 Asian financial crisis, which significantly affected Korea, was a key trigger behind the country's active pursuit of the FTA.

FTAs to Korea were perceived as necessary for survival. When former President Kim Dae-jung (DJ Administration) took office on 25 February 1998, the DJ administration inherited an economy that was shattered by the 1997 financial crisis. It also was pressed to carry out major structural reforms in almost every segment of the economy as a condition of a US $58.4 billion financial rescue package provided by the International Monetary Fund (IMF) which included pledges from the World Bank and Asian Development Bank as well as a second line of defence from G-7 countries. The major structural reforms mandated by the IMF consisted of restructuring the troubled financial institutions, improving corporate governance and enhancing labour market flexibility.[5] The IMF also demanded important external reforms. One of the top economic policy priorities of the DJ administration was centred on engaging with foreign companies to attract foreign direct investment (FDI) into Korea. In terms of trade liberalization, the DJ administration started with a series of FTA negotiations in 1998 with the aim of overcoming the currency crisis, strengthening the competitiveness of Korean industry and boosting exports (Ye 2017: 151).[6]

The role of FDI and FTAs throughout Korea's recent history of economic development has been, however, insignificant to say the least. In fact, the level of FDI/FTAs relative to the size of the economy had been negligible when compared to that of other countries in East Asia. This can be seen in a number of indicators. According to the United Nations Conference on Trade and Development's (UNCTAD) *World Investment Report 2006*, the inward FDI stock in Korea as a percentage of current GDP in 2005 was 8.0 per cent, above Japan (2.2 per cent) but below the levels of Taiwan (12.1 per cent), China (14.3 per cent) and Singapore (15. 8 per cent). What then has accounted for the relatively minor role played by FDI/FTAs in Korea's economic development in comparison to its Asian neighbours?

In the initial period of Korea's modern economic growth during the 1960s, the inflow of foreign capital was encouraged to make up for the shortage of domestic savings and foreign reserves. However, the Korean government preferred foreign borrowing, which brought foreign resources under its control. The general fear of Korean industries being dominated by foreign entities, which was deeply rooted in Korea's then recent history of Japanese colonization from 1910 to 1945, was too widespread inside Korea for the government to accommodate foreign management. Even today there is a lingering suspicion that FDI/FTAs are just a conduit through which foreigners/foreign countries can attempt to control Korean industries. While Korean leaders today show preferences towards FTAs, they face strong domestic interest groups and opposition (Ye 2017: 152). Notwithstanding, Korea has emerged in recent decades as one of the most active states in attracting FDI and pursuing FTAs with partners across the globe. Since the first bilateral FTA with Chile in 2004, over the past fourteen years (2004–2014), Korea has concluded fifteen FTAs with fifty-two countries, namely those with Chile, Singapore, EFTA (European FTA), ASEAN, India, the EU, Peru and the US and has recently concluded FTA negotiations and signed with Colombia, Turkey, Australia, New Zealand, Canada, China and Vietnam (see Table 5.3 for the detailed agreements). In addition, Korea is now negotiating with the GCC, Indonesia, Mexico, CJK and Japan for FTAs (refer to Table 5.3). At present the CJK economies have over thirty FTAs currently being negotiatied.

Ye (2017) has investigated Korea's international trade and FTA patterns from 1995 to 2012, using data on Korea's one hundred and twenty-two trading partners, and found that there were only two out of twenty-six FTAs in which Korea had pursued multilateral RTAs; and those two are still in a preliminary stage (Ye 2017: 151). Ravenhill (2003) pointed to three factors to explain the prevalent trend towards bilateral FTAs: (a) an increasing awareness of the weakness of existing regional institutions and initiatives; (b) perceptions of positive demonstration effects from regional agreements in other parts of the world; and (c) changing domestic economic interests after the economic crisis.

In the early years of Korea's pursuit of FTAs, four main FTA strategies dominated: pursuing simultaneous negotiations with interested counterpart countries, seeking comprehensive FTAs involving high levels of coverage and content (IPR, investment and services), undertaking national consensus building and driving FTAs with bigger markets (Ahn 2006). Governments of CJK declared that there is much to be gained from the CJK FTA which would eliminate both tariff and non-tariff barriers and ultimately lead to a common market.

> The strengthened trilateral relations will also contribute to making progress in the ongoing process of economic integration in East Asia, such as ASEAN+3, ASEAN+6, as well as the Asia-Pacific region. A CJK FTA would be regarded as a milestone in regional integration, fostering prosperity not only for the region but for the world as a whole.
>
> (DRC/NIRA/KIEP 2011: 146)

This (CJK FTA) could play and act as a major building block for the mega FTAs, namely RCEP and TPP. To Korea, the CJK FTA is not a new development but is the most important foreign policy over the past two decades. For example,

Table 5.3 Korea's FTAs (as of January 2017)

Classification	*Countries*	*Progress*	*Note*	*Significance*
In Effect (15 FTAs with 52 countries)	Chile	In Effect **1 April 2004**	Concluded in October 2002	First FTA concluded Bridge-head for Latin American market penetration
	Singapore	In Effect **2 March 2006**	Concluded in November 2004	Bridge-head for ASEAN market penetration
	EFTA	In Effect **1 September 2006**	Concluded in July 2005	Bridge-head for Europe market penetration
	ASEAN	In Effect **1 June 2007**	Goods: June 2007/Service: May 2009 Investment: September 2009/Whole: November 2010	First FTA with world's large economic bloc
	India	In Effect **1 January 2010**	Signed in August 2009	BRICs, huge market
	EU (twenty-eight countries)	In Effect **1 July 2011**	Signed in October 2010	World's largest economic bloc (based on GDP)
	Peru	In Effect **1 August 2011**	Signed in March 2011	Resource-affluent country Bridge-head for Latin American market penetration
	US	In Effect **15 March 2012**	Signed in June 2007 Additional negotiation concluded in December 2010	Huge and advanced economy
	Turkey	In Effect **1 May 2013**	Signed on Framework Agreement and Agreement on Trade in Goods in August 2012 (Service and Investment: Not in effect)	Bridge-head for Europe and Central Asia market penetration
	Australia	In Effect **12 December 2012**	Signed on 8 April 2014 Ratification of National Assembly in 2 December 2014	Resource-affluent country Major market in Oceania

(*Continued*)

Table 5.3 (Continued)

Classification	*Countries*	*Progress*	*Note*	*Significance*
	Canada	In Effect **1 January 2015**	Signed on 23 September 2014 Ratification of National Assembly in 2 December 2014	Advanced country of North America
	China	In Effect **20 December 2015**	Signed in 1 June 2015 Ratification of National Assembly in 30 November 2015	Largest trading partner of Korea (As of 2015)
	New Zealand	In Effect **20 December 2015**	Signed on 23 March 2015 Ratification of National Assembly in 30 November 2015	Major market in Oceania
	Vietnam	In Effect **20 December 2015**	Signed on 5 May 2015 Ratification of National Assembly in 30 November 2015	Third largest investment destination of Korea (As of September 2015)
	Colombia	In Effect **15 July 2016**	Ratification of National Assembly in 29 April 2014	Resource-affluent country Emerging market of Central and South American market
Under Negotiation (8 FTAs with 24 countries)	Korea·China·Japan	10th negotiation with chief delegates **June 2016**	11th negotiation to be held	Establishment of foundation for economic integration in Northeast Asia
	RCEP	16th negotiation **December 2016**	17th negotiation to be held	Contribution to economic integration in East Asia
	Six countries in Central America	Declaration of conclusion **November 2016**	Legal review to be scheduled in December 2016	Creating a new market in Central America
	Ecuador	5th negotiation **November 2016**	6th negotiation to be held	Resource-affluent country Bridge-head for Latin American market penetration
	Israel	2nd negotiation **December 2016**	3rd negotiation to be held	Model country for creative economy

	ASEAN – Revision	14th implementation committee **July 2016**	Under negotiation on the implementation committee schedule	Trade expansion and reflection of change in trade environment
	India – Revision	1st negotiation **October 2016**	2nd negotiation to be held	Granting preference to leading exports and improving origin criteria for trade expansion
	Chile – Revision	Declaration of negotiation initiation **November 2016**	1st negotiation to be held	Reflection of change in trade environment

Source: Korea FTA Portal (2017) (www.customs.go.kr/kcshome/site/index.do;jsessionid=86PthJLbXSrWnhDBJdyFvGpThrw4LbqH2kCLrYh3yKnJFSwd4ZRy!130641230?layoutSiteId=ftaportalkor) (accessed on 27 February 2018).

1 EFTA (four countries): Switzerland, Norway, Iceland, Liechtenstein.
2 ASEAN (ten10 countries): Brunei, Cambodia, Indonesia, Laos, Malaysia, Myanmar, the Philippines, Singapore, Vietnam, Thailand.
3 RCEP (Regional Comprehensive Economic Partnership): Korea, ten ASEAN member countries, China, Japan, India, Australia, New Zealand.
4 Six countries in Central America: Panama, Costa Rica, Guatemala, Honduras, El Salvador, Nicaragua.

when former President of Korea, Roh Moo-hyun came to power in 2003, one of the most important policy agendas was to enlarge and solidify the vision of the hub (Korea as an economic centre in Northeast Asia) launched by his predecessor (Kim Dae-jung). In fact, there were two specific policies for this goal by the Korean government, namely becoming the logistical and financial hub of Northeast Asia and concluding the CJK FTA.

Korea's real motivations for such an agreement remain unclear. Ravenhill (2003) suggests that the new interest in forming bilateralism among CJK is motivated by "an increasing awareness of the weakness of existing regional institutions and initiatives; perceptions of positive demonstration effects from regional agreements elsewhere; and changing configurations of domestic economic interests" (Ravenhill 2003: 299). In other words, given that Korea's export-oriented industrialization success has been dependent on WTO's multilateral trade negotiations, prolonged stagnant WTO trade negotiations (i.e. The Doha round)[7] have led Korea to prioritize regionalism and bilateralism.

The increasing awareness of the economic integration among CJK has been primarily driven by market forces rather than spearheaded by governments (Cai 2010: 102). For Korea, as indicated earlier, a CJK FTA is expected to lead to a positive economic effect. Unlike the case of China where political and diplomatic relationships appear to be the motive for the cross regional trade agreements, the economic imperative dominates Korea's FTA strategy. In particular, the main advantage of a CJK FTA is that China's eagerness in seeking a FTA with Korea and the huge Chinese domestic market with its rapid economic growth provides an opportunity to seek strong economic returns. This could include access to much-needed export markets such the EU, North America, ASEAN and China and an improvement in the nation's industrial and economic competitiveness (Koo 2010: 102). In turn, this will enhance Korea's position in CJK.

Korea's FTA strategy focuses on bilateral and extra-regional agreements (i.e. outside the Northeast and Southeast Asian regions). This new form of regionalism (bilateralism) is somewhat different from the gravity model of international trade theory that bilateral trade flows are proportional to their economy's size and their geographic distance. Park and Koo (2007) argue that the Japan-Singapore Economic Partnership Agreement signed in 2002, which is Japan's first post-World War II bilateral FTA, has also triggered a new interest in East Asia in shifting towards alternatives to the WTO-led multilateral trade agreements, targeting regions/partners both within and outside the region. Park and Koo (2007) observed that the Korea-Chile FTA, which came into force in 2004, was motivated by a number of important factors. These included economic opportunity gains, socio-economic restructuring after the 1997 financial crisis (refer to Chapter 3), a new consensus among policy makers that a new bilateral approach is not only complementary to the traditional export-oriented multilateral trade strategy but is also in line with the country's economic survival strategy in a rapidly changing world of regionalism, the emergence of Kim Dae Jung in 1998, which led the dramatic shift towards the neo-liberal FTA oriented international trade model and the ever-increasing peer competition and pressure motivating

Korea to negotiate bilateral FTA both within and outside East Asia. Park and Koo (2007: 267) further argued that:

> Aside from prospective economic gains, a major push factor for South Korea's policy shift toward FTAs was its change in political leadership and subsequent bureaucratic realignment. In pursuit of ambitious policy initiatives that intended to make South Korea a regional logistics hub and international business centre, President Kim Dae Jung was drawn to FTAs. For him, FTAs also held some political appeal because some non-competitive, politically sensitive sectors could be excluded from FTA negotiations, thus avoiding domestic resistance to trade liberalization.

Similarly, Korea's FTA shift from multilateralism to bilateral trade regionalism, was, according to Koo (2006), motivated by a number of strategic factors including:

- geographic focus beyond East Asia
- strengthening of economic security, securing of market access to major trading partners
- inclusion in a grand FTA road map of three different FTA partner groups, including immediate FTA partners (i.e. Chile, Singapore, EFTA and Japan), medium-term partners (i.e. Mexico, Canada, ASEAN and China) and long-term FTA partners (i.e. the US, EU and India)
- comprehensive FTAs (i.e. high-quality FTAs) covering not only trade in goods and services but also investment, government procurement, IPRs and technical standards.

A further important political motive for Korea's active involvement in cross-regionalism is to enhance the country's competitiveness and subsequently increase its international status and national image (Ye 2017). Solis and Katada (2007) offered a useful theoretical understanding of the origins and dynamics of this new form of East Asian cross-regionalism. In their study, they addressed three main questions: the role of regional factors, main objectives behind the selection of specific cross-regional partners and the impact of cross regional trade agreements on the intra-regional economic integration of CJK. In answering these questions, Solis and Katada (2007) adopted an eclectic approach in examining the motives behind cross-regionalism. They categorized three important motives behind the selection of cross-regional FTA partners: economic, security and leverage. Much of their economic (i.e. market access/expansion, avoidance of trade diversion) and security motives (i.e. reinforcement of security arrangements) analyses are commonly found in other literature on East Asian cross regionalism (e.g. Ye (2017), Koo (2006) and Park and Koo (2007)). The last category of motives termed by Solis and Katada (2007) is 'leverage motives'. According to Solis and Katana, the first leverage motive is 'capacity building'. The logic is that through the active engagement in FTA negotiations with more experienced counterparts (i.e. North America and the EU), the Korean government can enhance political leverage. In other words, simultaneous FTAs with large advanced economic powers (big markets) would enable Korea to achieve maximum economic benefits. Korea can also increase its international status and leverage by becoming a regional hub for international trade.

The second leverage motive according to Solis and Katada (2007) is 'creating precedents', which is related to domestic politics. The Government's strong commitment to the cross regional trade agreements (CRTAs) and preferential integration negotiations (FTAs) could lead the State to win its political battle over the domestic interest groups and to pave the way for wider and more vigorous international political-economic leverage in the CRTA diplomacy (Solis and Katada 2007: 250–251). The case of Korea and the US (KORUS) FTA demonstrates this leverage motive well. On 2 April 2007, KORUS concluded a landmark free trade agreement (FTA) after some fourteen months of negotiations. The IMF-mandated reform measures[8] resulting from the 1997 financial crisis have fallen short of tackling some of the practices that have been hobbling the Korean economy; namely, remaining restrictions to trade and investment, tightly protected farming market and limited access to a number of services, including financial, educational, health, legal and cultural categories. In short, the KORUS FTA has acted as a trigger for a second round of widespread market-opening measures needed ten years after the financial crisis of 1997.

The successful conclusion of KORUS and its subsequent ratification has also led to other successfully concluded agreements with larger trading partners such as the EU and China. Given that the trilateral negotiations have been slow, Korea's recently adopted dual track route (bilateral FTA) seems to be a more pragmatic approach. The recently signed (June 2015) and implemented (December 2015) Korea-China FTA clearly demonstrates this. For Korea, the CJK FTA and a bilateral FTA with China represents a heavily focused political-security and economy-driven model. It will also have a critical strategic value in providing enhanced leverage over North Korea. The CJK FTA would bring improved markets for Korean *chaebols*, increase the market for capital goods and offer increased investment opportunities.

Conclusion

Three factors – the state, society and markets – have been adopted in the Northeast Asian regional integration discussion (Ahn and Park 2007). While the motivation for integration is based on economic imperatives, the process of integration is clearly political. As was the case in European integration, coalition formation and leadership are now central aspects in the Northeast Asian integration (Laursen 2008: 5). While widening the membership of any agreement involves the extension of cooperation to more actors, deepening it can be more complex and controversial and will depend on whether the individual CJK countries seek to expand economic ties or whether they would want to secure the political gains from closer integration and cooperation. As Hoffmann (1966) argued in the case of the European Community (neo-functionalist view), "Every international system owes its inner logic and its unfolding to the diversity of domestic determinants, geo-historical situations and outside aims among its units" (Hoffmann 1966: 864). Therefore, strong and focused political leadership will be a prerequisite for successful, more complex and multi-party negotiations.

In an indirect way, the groundwork for such multi-party negotiations has been undertaken. Common partners exist between CJK countries in the individual bilateral signed agreements such as ASEAN, Chile, Peru, Singapore, Switzerland and Australia. The three countries have also participated in the RCEP negotiations in addition to the drawn-out CJK FTA negotiations. That this level of activity has not translated into more rapid progress on the CJK FTA, suggests that some of the political issues may be dominating at the moment. This can be seen in stark contrast to the recently concluded China-Korea FTA and the ongoing Japan-Korea FTA negotiations, which started in December 2003 and have been stalled since December 2004.

Notes

1 In 2015, 76 CJK companies (China: 37, Japan: 35, Korea: 4) were ranked among the top 500 companies by the Financial Times Global 500. These CJK companies account for US $412.1 billion in net income, US $4.7 trillion in market value and 8.4 million in employment worldwide (Trilateral Cooperation Secretariat 2017).

2 This information was gathered while we visited and discussed with members of the Chinese Academy of Social Sciences in Beijing, China in October 2012. The Chinese Government considers the FTA as a "new platform to further opening up to the outside and speeding up domestic reforms, an effective approach to integrate into global economy and strengthen economic cooperation with other economies, as well as particularly an important supplement to the multilateral trading system" (China FTA Network 2017).

3 Japan has interchangeably used the terms of EPA and FTA. Japan's EPA covers investment rules, trade facilitation measures, competition policy, and cooperation in technology transfer and intellectual property (Yoshimatsu 2008: 152).

4 The Japan-EU EPA will require Japan to eliminate tariffs on 94 per cent of all imports from the EU, including 82 per cent on farm and fishery products. In return the EU will be required to abolish tariffs on 99 per cent of imports from Japan and tariffs on Japanese vehicles in the eighth year after the pact is implemented and taxes on sake and green tea (*The Japan Times*, 9 December 2017).

5 In particular, the required reforms imposed by the IMF and found in other 1997 crisis affected countries such as Indonesia and Thailand, included hostile mergers and acquisitions (M&As), full opening of the domestic market to foreign products and massive restructuring of financial institutions and *chaebols* (i.e. a group of mostly family-owned and managed conglomerates in Korea such as Samsung, LG, SK and Hyundai). The IMF's rescue packages demanded a fundamental and major overhaul of the Korean political economy, which has been state- and *chaebol*-driven and brought issues such as transparency, accountability, corporate governance and lessened government intervention to the forefront of the local and foreign business community.

6 Under the guidance of the IMF since early 1998, the Korean economy rebounded from its late 1997 meltdown faster than expected. After falling nearly 7 per cent in 1998, real GDP was almost 11 per cent higher in 1999 and nearly 9 per cent higher

in 2000. Many neo-liberal supporters, such as international financial institutions, described Korea's economic recovery and financial stabilization as 'remarkable' (Crotty and Lee 2001: 183). For example, in 1999, investment expansion totalled US $2.3 billion, but in 2000, this figure rose more than fourfold to US $9.4 billion, comprising about 62 per cent of total FDI for the year 2000.

7 The Doha Round (also known as the Doha Development Agenda) is the latest round of trade negotiations among the WTO membership on twenty areas of trade through the introduction of lower trade barriers and revised trade rules. The Round was officially launched at the WTO's Fourth Ministerial Conference in Doha, Qatar, in November 2001. There have been a number of ministerial meetings held up until 2013 but the future of the Doha Round remains uncertain due to considerable differences and disagreements on the agriculture, industrial tariff and non-tariff barriers between the developing and developed countries (WTO 2017).

8 The most emphasized steps prescribed by the IMF to be taken by the Korean economy included:

- Fiscal adjustment that would include adjustments of the current account, redress of earlier public sector accesses and the guarantee of the correction of private sector excesses without unduly compressing domestic demand
- Firm monetary policy
- Restructuring weak financial sectors; closure of insolvent institutions; strengthening of regulation and supervision
- Improved public and corporate governance and increased transparency and accountability.

6 Economic integration in the wider East Asian region

Introduction

When the Asian financial crisis occurred in 1997, ASEAN played a key role in establishing a regional forum in East Asia by inviting the three Northeast Asian countries, namely, China, Japan and Korea to the ASEAN Summit meeting. Whilst such an invitation was designed to minimize the long-term impact of the crisis, it was also an opportunity for nations in East Asia to begin discussions on alternative forms of economic integration and cooperation. This chapter will explore these developments and place the CJK FTA negotiations within this broader context.

The beginning of economic regionalism in East Asia

ASEAN+3 process

The historic meeting of the leaders of ASEAN+3 (China, Japan and Korea) took place in Kuala Lumpur in December 1997. In 1998 at a meeting in Hanoi they decided to regularize such meetings with the ASEAN+3 Summit becoming an annual event. To support the Summit meetings, various ASEAN+3 ministerial meetings and Senior Officials meetings have taken place regularly since 2000. Thus, the ASEAN+3 framework in which East Asian countries could discuss cooperation issues among themselves was established.

At the Third ASEAN+3 Summit, held in Manila in November 1999, the leaders adopted the 'Joint Statement on East Asia Cooperation' in which they agreed to enhance this dialogue process and strengthen cooperation. The priority areas for collaboration at this stage addressed a variety of issues including economic cooperation, monetary and financial cooperation, social and human resources development, scientific and technical development, as well as political-security and transnational issues.

The East Asia Vision Group (EAVG) was created by the ASEAN+3 Summit in October 1999, and its report was submitted to the ASEAN+3 Summit in October 2001. The EAVG proposed the formation of an East Asian community, and in order to realize it, the Vision Group recommended the establishment of the East

Asian Free Trade Area (EAFTA). In addition, the Vision Group recommended the evolution of the annual meetings of ASEAN+3 into the East Asia Summit.[1] At the Fourth ASEAN+3 Summit in November 2000, the establishment of the East Asia Study Group (EASG 2002) was proposed, and its final report was adopted at the Sixth ASEAN+3 Summit held in Phnom Penh in November 2002. The final report of the EASG, drawn up by government officials, provided an assessment of the recommendations of the EAVG and an assessment of the implications of an East Asia Summit.

The EASG selected twenty-six implementable concrete measures with high priority: seventeen short-term measures including forming an East Asia Business Council, and nine medium-term and long-term measures, as well as a number of issues requiring further study. This latter group included forming an East Asian Free Trade Area and pursuing the evolution of the ASEAN+3 Summit into an East Asia Summit (EAS). Regarding the EAS, the EASG found that deeper integration of East Asian countries would be beneficial and desirable, but the EASG also stressed that the EAS should be part of an evolutionary and step-by-step process. The discussions have also revealed concerns that ASEAN may be marginalized if the transition towards an EAS moved too fast and noted the practical issue of whether an EAS would be encumbered with too many meetings.[2]

At the Eighth ASEAN+3 Summit held in Vientiane in November 2004, the leaders welcomed the decision by the ASEAN+3 Economic Ministers to set up an expert group to conduct a feasibility study on EAFTA, and they also supported ASEAN Leaders' decision to convene the first East Asia Summit (EAS) in Malaysia in 2005. At the Ninth ASEAN+3 Summit held in Kuala Lumpur on 12 December 2005, the leaders adopted the Kuala Lumpur Declaration on the ASEAN+3 Summit by reiterating their common long-term resolve to realize an East Asian community. The leaders shared the view that the EAS should be convened annually and that the EAS would play a significant role in the region. At the Eleventh ASEAN+3 Summit held in Singapore, in November 2007, the leaders adopted the "Second Joint Statement on East Asia Cooperation and APT (ASEAN+3) Cooperation Work Plan (2007–2017)". The documents provide strategic guidance for the future direction of APT cooperation. The Summit also endorsed the proposal to establish an "ASEAN Plus Three Cooperation Fund (APTCF)" to facilitate the implementation of the Work Plan. The Fund was launched during the Ninth APT Foreign Ministers' Meeting in July 2008 in Singapore.

Since the process began in 1997, ASEAN+3 cooperation has broadened and deepened. It includes cooperation in the areas of economics, finance, tourism, agricultural and forestry, energy, minerals, small and medium-sized enterprises, the environment, rural development and poverty eradication, social welfare, youth, women, civil service, labour, culture and arts, information and media, education, science, technology and innovation, public health, political and security matters and transnational crime. To handle such a broad agenda, sixty-eight mechanisms have been established to coordinate APT cooperation; these include: one summit, fifteen ministerial meetings, two hundred and twenty-two

Senior Officials, one Committee of Permanent Representatives to ASEAN+3, two Director-Generals, twenty-three technical-level and five other track meetings.[3]

East Asia Summit

As mentioned earlier, it was the EAVG that recommended the evolution of the annual meetings of ASEAN+3 into the East Asia Summit. The final report of the EASG noted two concerns: first, ASEAN may be marginalized if the transition towards an EAS moves too fast; second, EAS would be encumbered with too many meetings. ASEAN leaders seemed divided on the issue:

> Some ASEAN leaders suggested that community building could advance best through the ASEAN+3 framework, and thus the ASEAN+3 Summit could simply be converted into an East Asia Summit. Under this proposal, the thirteen ASEAN+3 members would chair the summit on a rotating basis. Other ASEAN leaders, however, contended that an expanded forum would dilute the voices of ASEAN nations, which are much weaker entities than their Northeast Asian partners.
>
> (Tanaka 2006: 1)

Then, at the Tenth ASEAN Summit in November 2004, ASEAN leaders decided to continue the ASEAN+3 Summit and hold a separate East Asia Summit. Consequently, the First East Asia Summit was held on 14 December 2005 in Kuala Lumpur, Malaysia. It was attended by the Heads of State/Government of ASEAN, Australia, China, India, Japan, Korea and New Zealand. Russia was invited as Guest of the Government of Malaysia.

Although the idea of the EAS came from the ASEAN+3 process, this newly born EAS differed significantly from the EAS recommended by the EAVG and EASG. The first difference lies in its membership, which includes three additional countries to the ASEAN+3 countries. Second, ASEAN centrality is maintained: the EAS will be hosted and chaired by an ASEAN member country that assumes the ASEAN Chairmanship and will be held back-to-back with the annual ASEAN Summit, precisely like the ASEAN+3 process. Finally, the new EAS is a separate forum, while the original idea of EAS was the evolution of ASEAN+3 summits. Thus, among the concerns raised at the EASG, the fear of weakening the ASEAN centrality was resolved; however, the practical issue of whether an EAS would be encumbered with too many meetings probably became more complicated with the creation of an additional forum.

According to the Kuala Lumpur Declaration on the East Asia Summit, the EAS was established as a forum for dialogue on broad strategic, political and economic issues of common interest and concern with the aim of promoting peace, stability and economic prosperity in East Asia. It would be an open, inclusive, transparent and outward-looking forum in which the member countries strive to strengthen global norms and universally recognized values with ASEAN as the driving force, working in partnership with the other participants of the East Asia Summit. Viewed from the declarations or statements issued during the East Asia Summits from 2005 to 2015, the major issues discussed at the EAS have been: (a) prevention of infectious diseases (avian influenza prevention, control and response in 2005, regional responses to malaria control and addressing resistance to antimalarial medicines in 2012, regional response to the Ebola virus in 2014, enhancing regional health security relating to infectious diseases with epidemic and pandemic potential in 2015); (b) security and transnational crime (the rise of violence and brutality committed by terrorist organizations in Iraq and Syria in 2014, combating wildlife trafficking in 2014, countering violent extremism in 2015, issues related to security of and the use of information and communications technology in 2015); (c) energy security and environment protection (East Asian energy security in 2007 in the Philippines, climate change, energy and the environment in 2007 in Singapore); (4) natural disaster mitigation (disaster management in 2009, rapid disaster response in 2014); and (5) development (development initiative in 2012, food security in 2013).

Despite concerns of weakening ASEAN centrality, there was a new development in terms of membership. The US and Russia became new members, participating for the first time in the Sixth EAS held in Bali in November 2011. Previously, at the Fifth East Asia Summit (EAS), held in Vietnam in October 2010, the Russian Foreign Minister and the US Secretary of State, who represented their respective Presidents, had been invited as special guests of the Chair.

Proliferation of FTAs in East Asia

The first RTA concluded among Asia-Pacific countries was the Asia-Pacific Trade Agreement (APTA),[4] which was signed by Bangladesh, India, Korea, Laos and Sri Lanka in 1975 and came into effect in June 1976. The Laos-Thailand Preferential Trading Arrangement was concluded in 1991. These two agreements were reported to the GATT as preferential trade agreements under the Enabling Clause. Additionally, the AFTA was signed among six ASEAN countries, namely, Brunei, Indonesia, Malaysia, Philippines, Singapore and Thailand, in January 1992. Vietnam joined in 1995, Laos and Myanmar in 1997 and Cambodia in 1999. The AFTA was also reported under the Enabling Clause but reported to the GATT as a FTA.

At the turn of the century, East Asian countries joined the global trend towards regionalism by concluding FTAs under GATT Article 24. The New Zealand-Singapore Closer Economic Partnership came into effect in January 2001 and the Japan-Singapore Economic Agreement for a New-Age Partnership came into effect in November 2002. This was followed by numerous FTAs involving East Asian countries, within the region and beyond. Most ASEAN countries, except for Singapore, have concluded FTAs primarily with regional countries, while Korea, China, Japan as well as India and Australia have also concluded a number of FTAs with non-regional partners.

Among the many FTAs concluded by regional countries, it is noteworthy that ASEAN has concluded FTAs with China, Korea, Japan, as well as Australia-New Zealand and India. ASEAN signed the Trade in Goods Agreement (November 2004), Trade in Services Agreement (January 2007) and Investment Agreement (August 2009) with China. ASEAN also signed separately the Trade in Goods Agreement (August 2006), Trade in Services Agreement (November 2007) and the Investment Agreement (June 2009) with Korea. With Japan, ASEAN signed the Comprehensive Economic Partnership Agreement in June 2008. In addition, the ASEAN-Australia and New Zealand FTA was signed in February 2009, and ASEAN-India Trade in Goods Agreement was signed in August 2009.

Singapore has concluded bilateral FTAs with all regional countries, in addition to its FTAs under ASEAN. As discussed earlier, the three Northeast Asian countries formed many bilateral FTAs with regional countries in addition to their FTAs with ASEAN. Japan concluded bilateral FTAs with ASEAN+6 members and Vietnam, as well as with India and Australia. Korea concluded bilateral FTAs with Singapore, India, Australia, China, New Zealand and Vietnam. China concluded bilateral FTAs with New Zealand, Singapore, Korea, Australia and Thailand. Additionally, other bilateral FTAs concluded involving ASEAN members include the Thailand-Australia FTA, Thailand-New Zealand FTA, Thailand-India FTA, Malaysia-New Zealand FTA, Malaysia-India FTA and Malaysia-Australia. The only FTA concluded between ASEAN dialogue partners not listed above is the Closer Economic Relations (CER) between Australia and New Zealand.[5] In addition, when other economies in the region are included, the list of concluded FTAs extends to the China-Hong Kong Closer Economic Partnership Arrangement (CEPA), China-Macao CEPA and New Zealand-Hong Kong Closer Economic Partnership Agreement and China-Taipei Economic Cooperation Framework Agreement.[6] Such a complex web of FTAs among the East Asian countries resulted partly from ASEAN dialogue partners also concluding separate bilateral FTAs with some individual ASEAN members on top of their FTAs with ASEAN.

Search for a region-wide FTA in East Asia

As noted above, at the ASEAN+3 Summit in October 2001, the East Asia Vision Group (EAVG) submitted its report titled, "Towards an East Asian Community: Region of Peace, Prosperity and Progress", which recommended the establishment of an East Asian Free Trade Area (EAFTA). In November 2002, the East Asia Study Group (EASG) also proposed the formation of an EAFTA. In 2004, ASEAN Economic Ministers (AEM) together with the economic ministers from China, Japan and Korea (AEM+3) decided to set up an expert group initiated by China to conduct a feasibility study on an EAFTA. This step was welcomed by leaders at the Eighth ASEAN+3 Summit held in Vientiane in November 2004. The Joint Expert Group reported the outcome of the study to AEM+3 in

August 2006. Korea subsequently proposed a follow-up in-depth study, which was welcomed by leaders at the Tenth ASEAN+3 Summit in January 2007. The outcome of the EAFTA Phase II Study was presented at the AEM+3 Consultations in Bangkok on 15 August 2009.

At the Second East Asia Summit (EAS) held in Cebu, Philippines, in January 2007, leaders also agreed to launch a Track Two study on Comprehensive Economic Partnership in East Asia (CEPEA). This was initiated by the Japanese government and involved experts from sixteen countries to deepen integration. The outcome of the Track Two study on CEPEA was also presented at the AEM+3 Consultations in Bangkok on 15 August 2009. The Ministers welcomed the final reports of both EAFTA and CEPEA and, on the basis of their recommendations, the Ministers agreed to upgrade the joint study for a region-wide FTA in East Asia conducted by the region's experts to government-level discussions by establishing working groups on rules of origin, tariff nomenclature, customs-related issues and economic cooperation. Later, this decision was confirmed at the Twelfth ASEAN+3 Summit and the fourth East Asia Summit held in Cha-am Hua Hin, Thailand, in October 2009. The process of forming a region-wide FTA in East Asia, which began after the Asian financial crisis, appears to have gained important momentum in the wake of the Global Financial Crisis. However, due to the different positions between China and Japan regarding the initial participating countries in the working groups, ASEAN+3 vs. ASEAN+6, the process of forming a region-wide FTA in East Asia was delayed.

Regional Comprehensive Economic Partnership (RCEP)

Emergence of the RCEP and its negotiations

In November 2011, ASEAN leaders agreed to establish an ASEAN-led process by setting out principles under which ASEAN will engage interested ASEAN FTA partners in establishing a region-wide FTA (i.e. ASEAN Framework for Regional Comprehensive Economic Partnership (RCEP)). ASEAN had thus finally decided to take the leadership role in establishing a region-wide FTA. Following the ASEAN leaders' agreement in April 2012 to announce the launch of the RCEP negotiations at the next summit meeting, the leaders of sixteen East Asian countries declared the start of RCEP negotiations in Phnom Penh on 20 November 2012. ASEAN's decision to launch the RCEP seemed to have been motivated by three factors. First, as mentioned above, the process of forming a region-wide FTA in East Asia was delayed due to the discord between China and Japan. Second, given the possibility of forming a FTA among the three Northeast Asian countries, namely the China-Japan-Korea FTA, ASEAN is likely to have felt the need to take the initiative for a region-wide FTA in East Asia. Third, the fast-moving Trans-Pacific Partnership (TPP) became a major competitor to a region-wide FTA in East Asia and could also be a dividing factor among ASEAN countries, since four ASEAN members (Singapore, Brunei, Malaysia and Vietnam) had already decided to participate in the TPP.

The first round of RCEP negotiations was held in Bandar Seri Begawan, Brunei, on 9–13 May 2013. At the first meeting, the participating countries discussed the basic framework of negotiations. They agreed to form working groups on Trade in Goods, Services, Investment and Other Issues and that the Trade Negotiating Committee (TNC) would be responsible for overall coordination of issues and making decisions. The second round of RCEP negotiations took place in Brisbane, Australia, on 23–27 September 2013. The third round of negotiations was held in Kuala Lumpur, Malaysia, on 20–24 January 2004 and the fourth round took place in Nanning, China, on 31 March-3 April 2014. The fifth round of talks was held in Singapore on 23–27 June 2014, while the sixth round took place in New Delhi, India on 1–5 December 2014. The seventh round of negotiations was held in Bangkok, Thailand, on 9–13 February 2015, while the eighth round of talks took place in Kyoto, Japan, on 8–13 June 2015. The ninth round of negotiations was held in Nay Pyi Taw, Myanmar on 3–7 August 2015 and the tenth round of negotiations took place in Busan, Korea on 12–16 October 2015.

Meanwhile, four RCEP Ministerial Meetings have been held. The first RCEP Ministerial Meeting took place in Bandar Seri Begawan, Brunei, on 19 August 2013, while the second RCEP Ministerial Meeting was held in Nay Pyi Taw, Myanmar, on 27 August 2014. The RCEP Intersessional Ministerial Meeting and third RCEP Ministerial Meeting took place in Kuala Lumpur, Malaysia, on 10 July and 21 August 2015, respectively. Although the negotiations were supposed to be completed by 2015, the leaders of the RCEP participating countries issued a Joint Statement on the RCEP Negotiations in Kuala Lumpur on 22 November in which they instructed their Ministers and negotiators to conclude the RCEP negotiations in 2016. As of the tenth round of negotiations, apart from the TNC, fourteen working groups were established covering areas such as trade in goods, trade in services, investment, economic and technical cooperation, competition, intellectual property, legal and institutional issues, SPS measures, TBT, rules of origin, electronic commerce, customs-related issues, financial services and telecommunications. In 2016, the eleventh round of negotiations was held in Brunei on 15–19 February, the twelfth round of negotiations took place in Perth, Australia, on 24–29 April 2016 and the thirteenth round of negotiations was held in Auckland, New Zealand, on 10–18 June 2016.

Challenges for the RCEP

The RCEP aims to be a comprehensive, high-quality and mutually beneficial economic partnership agreement among the ASEAN member states and ASEAN's FTA partners. In addition, taking into consideration the different levels of development, the RCEP is supposed to include provisions on special and differential treatment to developing ASEAN member states, plus additional flexibility to the least-developed ASEAN member states. The most fundamental obstacle is the diversity among East Asian countries. Table 6.1 indicates clearly the existing diversities among East Asian countries in terms of the size of population

Table 6.1 Diversity among East Asian countries (as of 2014)

	Population (Millions)	*GDP (Billions of US$)*	*Per Capita GDP (US$)*
Brunei	0.4	15.0	35,376
Cambodia	15.3	16.4	1,067
Indonesia	255.5	848.0	3,354
Laos	6.7	11.7	1,692
Malaysia	29.9	326.1	10,803
Myanmar	53.4	67.6	1,259
Philippines	99.1	285.1	2,848
Singapore	5.5	301.2	54,593
Thailand	67.7	405.5	6,033
Vietnam	92.4	186.6	2,016
China	1,369.4	10,066.7	7,223
Japan	126.8	4,586.7	36,116
Korea	50.1	1,415.9	28,598
Australia	23.6	1,474.8	62,414
New Zealand	4.5	202.2	44,420
India	1,295.3	2,041.1	1,610

Source: UNCTAD (2015), Statistics (accessed on 20 June 2016).

and economy as well as the level of economic development. In particular, the substantial gap in per capita GDP between Australia (US $62,414), Singapore (US $54,593), New Zealand (US $44,420), Japan (US $36,116) and Brunei (US $35,376), on the one hand, and Cambodia (US $1,067), Myanmar (US $1,259), India (US $1,610) and Laos (US $1,692), on the other, has constituted a serious obstacle to forming a high-level FTA.

Second, since ASEAN concluded five ASEAN+1 FTAs with China, Japan, Korea, India and Australia-New Zealand, these FTAs would be valuable for the RCEP negotiations. However, a closer look at the existing ASEAN+1 FTAs reveals that despite some elements that would be helpful to consolidating the five ASEAN+1 FTAs, the consolidation process would not be easy. Table 6.2 shows the trade liberalization rate, defined as the proportion of tariff lines (number of products) subject to tariff elimination among total number of tariff lines for five ASEAN+1 FTAs. The last row of the table shows the average trade liberalization rates for the five ASEAN+1 FTAs. The AANZFTA has the highest trade liberalization rate at 95.7 per cent, while the AIFTA has the lowest rate at 79.6 per cent. Indeed, the trade liberalization rate for AIFTA is exceptionally low compared to those for other ASEAN+1 FTAs, whose rates are greater than 90 per cent.

It should be noted that many ASEAN countries have different trade liberalization commitments depending on ASEAN's FTA partners. One noticeable pattern is very low trade liberalization rates in the AIFTA. Indonesia registered a very low trade liberalization rate of 48.6 per cent. Given the low level of service and investment liberalization in the existing ASEAN+1 FTAs, their consolidation will not be enough to achieve a high-level RCEP in terms of liberalization. Moreover, the consolidation among ASEAN+1 FTAs will not be enough to form an RCEP,

Table 6.2 Level of liberalization by country under the ASEAN+1 FTAs (%)

Country	*AANZFTA*	*ACFTA*	*AIFTA*	*AJCEP*	*AKFTA*	*Average*
Brunei	99.2	98.3	85.3	97.5	99.1	95.9
Cambodia	89.1	89.9	88.4	85.1	90.8	88.7
Indonesia	93.1	92.3	48.6	91.2	91.1	83.3
Laos	91.8	97.4	80.1	86.3	90.0	89.1
Malaysia	97.3	92.6	79.7	93.9	92.4	91.2
Myanmar	88.1	93.6	76.6	84.9	91.6	86.9
Philippines	95.1	92.5	80.9	97.1	89.6	91.1
Singapore	100	100	100	100	100	100
Thailand	98.9	93.5	78.1	96.4	95.1	92.4
Vietnam	94.8	92.2	79.5	94.2	89.3	90.0
Australia	100					
China		94.7				
Indonesia			78.8			
Japan				91.9		
Korea					90.4	
New Zealand	100					
Average	95.6	94.3	79.6	92.6	92.7	90.9

Source: Yoshifumi Fukunaga and Arata Kuno (May 2012).

Notes: AANZFTA: ASEAN-Australia-New Zealand FFTA, ACFTA: ASEAN-China FTA, AIFTA: ASEAN-India FTA, AJCEP: ASEAN-Japan CEP, AKFTA: ASEAN-Korea FTA. The share of duty free tariff lines after the transition period is based on the HS six-digit level of the HS2007 version. The following tariff schedules are originally based on the HS2002 version and converted into HS 2007: Indonesia in the AANZFTA, Laos in the ACFTA, all ASEAN Member States in AJCEP and Brunei, Malaysia and the Philippines in AKFTA.

because there remain six bilateral missing links among ASEAN FTA partners: China-Japan, China-India, Japan-Korea, Japan-New Zealand, India-Australia and India-New Zealand (see Figure 6.1).

It would be difficult to form a comprehensive and high-quality FTA within a relatively short period of time among sixteen countries whose levels of economic development vary significantly. Furthermore, the formation of the RCEP could be affected by the revised Trans-Pacific Partnership (CPTPP), which was signed by the remaining eleven countries in 2018, although it is not scheduled to come into effect until 2019. Out of sixteen countries participating in the RCEP negotiations, seven of them, Singapore, Brunei, New Zealand, Australia, Vietnam, Malaysia and Japan, have joined the CPTPP. So, when the CPTPP comes into effect, some of the countries participating in RCEP who are also APEC members, namely Thailand, the Philippines, Indonesia, Korea and China, may be tempted to join the CPTPP. In fact, many of these countries have already expressed their intention to join the old TPP. Given that the CPTPP is quite comprehensive and a high-quality FTA, if a growing number of countries joins the CPTPP, the RCEP's rationale could be obsolete. Consequently, the CPTPP, which is a guide for the Free Trade Area of the Asia-Pacific (FTAAP), is likely to weaken the RCEP. The extent to which this may happen

	ASEAN	China	Japan	Korea	India	Australia
China	•					
Japan	•	–				
Korea	•	•				
India	•	–	•	•		
Australia	•	•	•	•	–	
New Zealand	•	•	–	•	–	•

Sources*:* Asia Regional Integration Centre (http://aric.adb.org/fta-country); Ministry of Commerce of the People's Republic of China, China FTA Network, (http://fta.mofcom.gov.cn/english/index.shtml); Ministry of Foreign Affairs of Japan, Free Trade Agreement and Economic Partnership Agreement (www.mofa.go.jp/policy/economy/fta/index.html); Ministry of Trade, Industry and Energy of the Republic of Korea (http://fta.go.kr/main/situation/kfta/ov/).

Figure 6.1 FTAs among East Asian countries

is, however, speculative at this moment given that the long-term intentions of the US are unknown.

Lastly, one of the main reasons for forming a region-wide FTA such as the RCEP, is to overcome the 'Spaghetti Bowl Phenomenon' caused by the proliferation of bilateral and plurilateral FTAs with different rules of origin and tariff schedules. So far, the RCEP does not appear to be a replacement for the existing bilateral and plurilateral FTAs. In that sense, it could become rather a symbolic region-wide FTA in East Asia, should it coexist along with many high-quality bilateral and plurilateral FTAs.

Leadership

ASEAN has assumed a leading role in terms of economic integration in East Asia. First, the AFTA Agreement was signed by ASEAN+6 countries in January 1992. ASEAN was also instrumental in the proliferation of FTAs in East Asia by forming five ASEAN+1 FTAs with China, Japan, Korea, India and Australia-New Zealand. Thus, ASEAN has become the hub of East Asian FTA networks and has set the basic framework for the construction of a region-wide East Asian FTA. It was on the basis of these ASEAN+1 FTAs that both the Joint Expert Group for EAFTA and CEPEA Tract II Study Group attempted to build regional FTAs. In November 2011, ASEAN finally took the leadership role for the establishment of a region-wide FTA in East Asia by proposing the ASEAN Framework for the

Regional Comprehensive Economic Partnership (RCEP). However, during the RCEP negotiations, ASEAN's leadership has not been highly visible. This is to be contrasted with the strong leadership of the US in the former TPP negotiations.

The three Northeast Asian countries could provide a certain level of leadership. It was the former Chinese Premier Zhu Rong-ji who first proposed an ASEAN-China FTA, followed by similar proposals from Japan and Korea. Thus, China, Japan and Korea have played a more active role than ASEAN in the process of forming ASEAN+1 FTAs. As mentioned earlier, China and Korea took the initiative for the EAFTA studies conducted by experts from ASEAN+3 countries, while the CEPEA study conducted by experts from ASEAN+6 countries, was led by Japan. Until the conclusion of ASEAN+1 FTAs, and during the course of joint studies on a region-wide FTA in East Asia among regional experts, China, Japan and Korea have assumed an active leadership role, even though it could be argued that these initiatives were motivated to a greater extent by regional geo-political dynamics than regional economic integration rationales.

The competition among the three Northeast Asian countries, which had played a positive role up to the conclusion of ASEAN+1 FTAs, has turned into a major stumbling block in terms of the advancement of a region-wide FTA. As discussed earlier, the working groups could not function properly as arguments occurred over the ASEAN+3 vs. ASEAN+6 proposal. Furthermore, since the negotiations for both the RCEP and CJK FTA have proceeded simultaneously from 2013, the three countries have had an opportunity to assume a positive role to accelerate economic integration in East Asia. Two ways are open for fulfilling this role. First, the countries can actively participate in the negotiations of the RCEP led by ASEAN. In addition, the countries can indirectly lead the RCEP negotiations by accelerating the CJK FTA negotiations. Should these three countries decide to proceed rapidly with the CJK FTA negotiations, they would be setting an example for the RCEP negotiations. China, Japan and Korea should have the RCEP negotiations in mind when they conduct the CJK FTA negotiations. However, so far, the three countries have failed to form a CJK FTA in time to lead the RCEP process, and thus have become obstacles rather than leaders.

Beyond the RCEP: East Asian Economic Community

In line with efforts for liberalizing intra-ASEAN trade in goods, trade in services and investment, ASEAN has begun a more comprehensive and deeper integration process. At the Bali ASEAN Summit Meeting, which was held in October 2003, the leaders agreed to establish the ASEAN Community by 2020 as outlined in ASEAN Vision 2020, and the target year was moved forward to 2015 at the Cebu ASEAN Summit Meeting in January 2007. In November 2007, the Declaration on the ASEAN Economic Community Blueprint was adopted. The ASEAN Economic Community (AEC) envisages (a) a single market and production base, (b) a highly competitive economic region, (c) a region of equitable economic development and (d) a region fully integrated into the global economy. The AEC was to be established at the end of 2015.

The vision of establishing an East Asian Community was first proposed by the EAVG at the ASEAN+3 Summit in October 2001. After a decade since the EAVG submitted its report, the East Asia Vision Group II (EAVG II) was established in October 2011 to review the ASEAN+3 cooperation over the past fifteen years and provide a future vision of the ASEAN+3 for the coming decades. The EAVG II Report was submitted to the Fifteenth ASEAN+3 Commemorative Summit in Phnom Penh on November 2012.

The EAVG II recommended the realization of an East Asia Economic Community by 2020 as the main pillar of the new vision. The East Asia Economic Community would be composed of four key elements: (a) single market and production base, (b) financial stability, food and energy security, (c) equitable and sustainable development and (d) constructive contribution to the global economy.

Economic status and intra-regional dependency

Economic status of East Asia and share of China, Japan and Korea

Over the past twenty-five years, the share of East Asia (ASEAN+6) in the world's GDP has markedly increased. It rose from 20.8 per cent in 1990 to 30.6 per cent in 2015 (see Figure 6.2).[7] On the other hand, during the same period, the share of China, Japan and Korea in East Asia's total GDP decreased from 78.0 per cent to 73.6 per cent (see Figure 6.3).

The share of East Asia in the world's total exports grew from 17.9 per cent in 1990 to 30.8 per cent in 2015, while its share in the world's total imports rose from 16.6 per cent in 1990 to 26.8 per cent in 2015. During the same period, the shares of China, Japan and Korea in East Asia's total exports and total imports rose slightly from 66.2 per cent to 67.2 per cent and from 60.2 per cent to 61.6 per cent respectively.[8]

As for FDI, the share of East Asia in the world's total inward FDI rose from 14.1 per cent in 1990 to 29.6 per cent in 2014, whereas its share in the world's total outward FDI increased from 23.6 per cent in 1990 to 25.9 per cent in 2014. In the same period, the share of China, Japan and Korea in East Asia's total inward FDI surged from 19.0 per cent to 75.3 per cent, while their share in East Asia's total outward FDI diminished from 91.5 per cent to 74.4 per cent.[9] Table 6.3 indicates that in 2014, in terms of GDP, the RCEP's share (28.7 per cent) was larger than that of NAFTA (26.6 per cent) and the EU (23.9 per cent). In terms of trade, RCEP's share was larger than that of NAFTA but smaller than that of the EU, while in terms of inward FDI, the RCEP's share was larger than that of the EU and NAFTA. In the case of outward FDI, the RCEP's share was smaller than that of NAFTA but larger than that of the EU. Overall, the RCEP's economic status was comparable to that of the EU and NAFTA.

Compared to the proposed TPP, the RCEP's share was smaller than that of the TPP in terms of GDP and outward FDI, but higher than that of the TPP

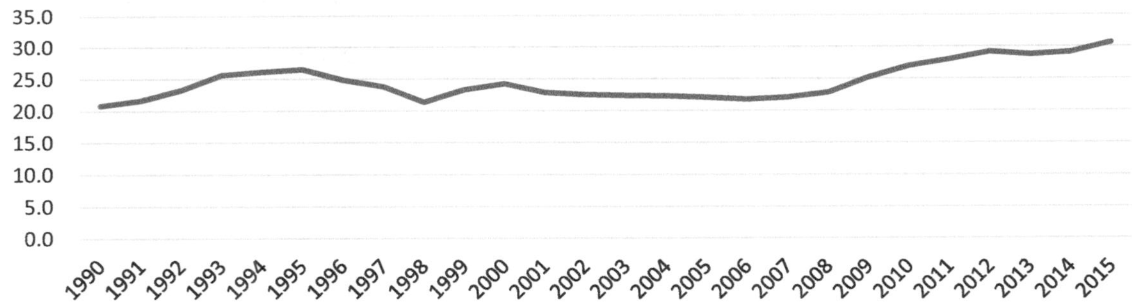

Figure 6.2 East Asia's share in the world's GDP (%)

Source: IMF, World Economic Outlook 2016 (accessed on 3 June 2016).

Figure 6.3 The share of China-Japan-Korea in East Asia's total GDP (%)

Source: IMF, World Economic Outlook 2016 (accessed on 3 June 2016).

Table 6.3 Economic status of East Asia and other major economic regions (2014) (share in world's total GDP, %)

	CJK	*RCEP*	*NAFTA*	*EU (28)*	*TPP*
Population	21.3	48.1	6.7	7.0	11.2
GDP	20.7	28.7	26.6	23.9	36.3
Exports	19.0	29.0	13.1	32.4	23.1
Imports	16.9	27.8	17.4	31.7	27.6
Inward FDI	11.4	29.6	13.8	21.0	28.1
Outward FDI	19.3	25.9	29.2	20.8	42.9

Source: UNCTAD (2015), Statistics (accessed on 20 June 2016).

in terms of exports, while the share was about the same in terms of imports and inward FDI.

Intra-regional trade among East Asian countries

Intra-regional trade dependencies of East Asia

Functional economic integration seems to have proceeded relatively smoothly in East Asia. East Asian countries thus are currently much more dependent on one another in terms of trade than twenty-five years ago. As shown in Figure 6.4, the share of intra-regional trade in East Asia (ASEAN+6 countries) has in general increased between 1990 and 2015. It increased from 33.0 per cent in 1990 to 40.9 per cent in 1996 before decreasing to 37.1 per cent in 1998 as a result of the Asian financial crisis; it then rose to 44.2 per cent in 2010 before reaching 43.4 per cent in 2015. The upsurge in the share of intra-regional trade in East Asia seems more evident, when it is compared to that of NAFTA and the EU. The share of intra-regional trade of ASEAN+6 countries (33.0 per cent) was lower than that of NAFTA (37.3 per cent) in 1990, whereas the share of intra-regional trade of ASEAN+6 (43.4 per cent) was higher than that of NAFTA (41.1 per cent) in 2015.

Furthermore, the dependence on intra-regional trade in East Asia is clearly illustrated when Hong Kong and Taiwan (HT) are also included. The shares of intra-regional trade among ASEAN+6+HT rose from 44.5 per cent in 1990 to 54.7 per cent in 2015. It is also notable that the share of intra-regional trade of ASEAN+6+HT was much lower than that of the EU-15 (64.7 per cent) in 1990 but exceeded that of the EU-15 (52.6 per cent) in 2015. Thus, as of 2015 the share of intra-regional trade of East Asia narrowly defined was higher than that of NAFTA, whereas the share of intra-regional trade of East Asia broadly defined was higher than that of the EU-15.

However, when analysed in terms of the simple concentration ratio, East Asia's functional economic integration proceeded smoothly only up to 2001, after which the intra-regional trade intensity in East Asia declined. East Asia's simple

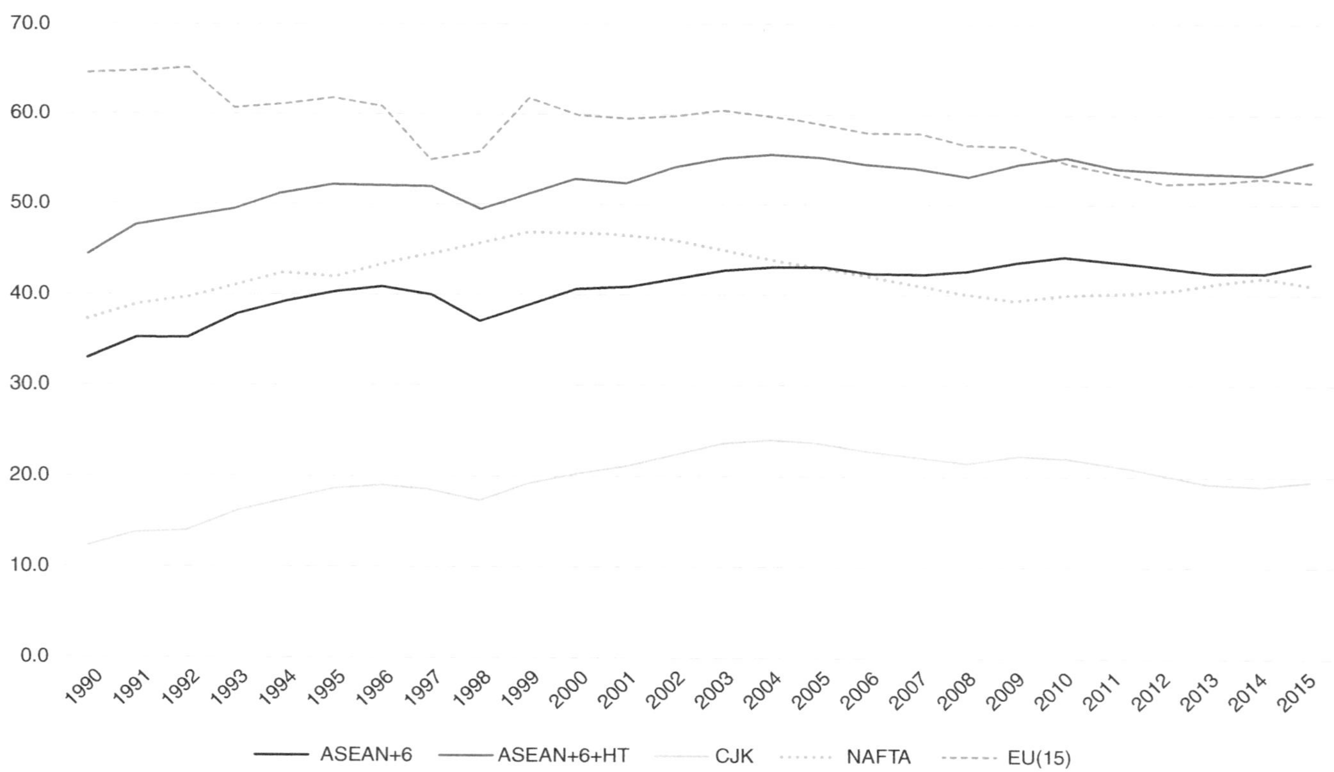

Figure 6.4 Shares of intra-regional trade in East Asia and other major economic regions (%)

Source: Calculated from IMF (2015), DOTS Database; Taiwan Bureau of Foreign Trade, Trade Statistics (accessed on 30 June 2016).

concentration ratio increased from 1.82 in 1990 to 1.98 in 2001 before diminishing to 1.48 in 2015. Consequently, it was higher than that of the EU-15 until 2009 but has been lower than that of the EU-15 since 2002. Thus, in 2015, East Asia's simple concentration ratio was lower than that of NAFTA (2.48) and the EU (1.88), but higher than that of CJK (1.04) (see Figure 6.5).

The regional introversion index of East Asian countries (Figure 6.6) shows a similar pattern to the simple concentration ratio. Figures rose from 0.48 in 1990 to 0.59 in 2003 before falling to 0.41 in 2014 and rebounding to 0.43 in 2015. Over the past twenty-five years, the index has been higher than that of CJK, but in general lower than that of the EU and NAFTA, meaning that the bias towards intra-regional trade of East Asian countries has been stronger than that of CJK, but mostly weaker than that of the EU and NAFTA. In 2015, East Asia's regional introversion index was much higher than that of CJK (0.03), but substantially lower than that of the EU (0.66) and NAFTA (0.68).

Trade inter-dependency among East Asian countries

The intra-regional trade dependency level of East Asian countries increased in twelve out of sixteen East Asian countries between 1990 and 2015, while it fell in four East Asian countries, namely, Brunei, Cambodia, Malaysia and Indonesia (see Table 6.4). Despite the generally rising trend of trade inter-dependency among East Asian countries, the level of intra-regional trade dependency differs greatly from country to country. Overall, ASEAN countries' intra-regional trade dependency was higher than that of China, Japan and Korea. In 2015, the intra-regional trade dependency was very high in Laos (97.4 per cent) and Myanmar (93.7 per cent) and relatively high in Singapore (67.5 per cent), Cambodia (63.0 per cent), Vietnam (61.2 per cent), Indonesia (58.5 per cent), Thailand (56.7 per cent) and Malaysia (50.4 per cent).

Figures for 2015 show that, among the Northeast Asian countries, China had the lowest intra-regional trade dependency (31.7 per cent), and Korea had the highest (47.0 per cent), while Japan's intra-regional trade dependency increased the most over the past twenty-five years (from 5.7 per cent to 46.5 per cent). As for Australia (66.9 per cent) and New Zealand (57.5 per cent), the intra-regional trade dependency was higher than that of the Northeast Asian countries, whereas India had the lowest (27.3 per cent) intra-regional trade dependency level among the East Asian countries.

Three significant conclusions can be drawn from Table 6.4 regarding East Asian countries' trade dependency on China, Japan and Korea. First, East Asian countries, with the exception of Brunei, Indonesia and Malaysia, have recorded increased levels of trade dependency on CJK over the period 1990 to 2015. In fact, all East Asian countries saw their trade dependency on CJK rise to a higher level in 2015 compared to 1990. Second, for a majority of East Asian countries, trade dependency on CJK was higher than their trade dependency on ASEAN. In 2015, the trade dependency on CJK was higher than that on ASEAN for all East Asian countries except for Cambodia, Laos and Singapore. Third, there has been

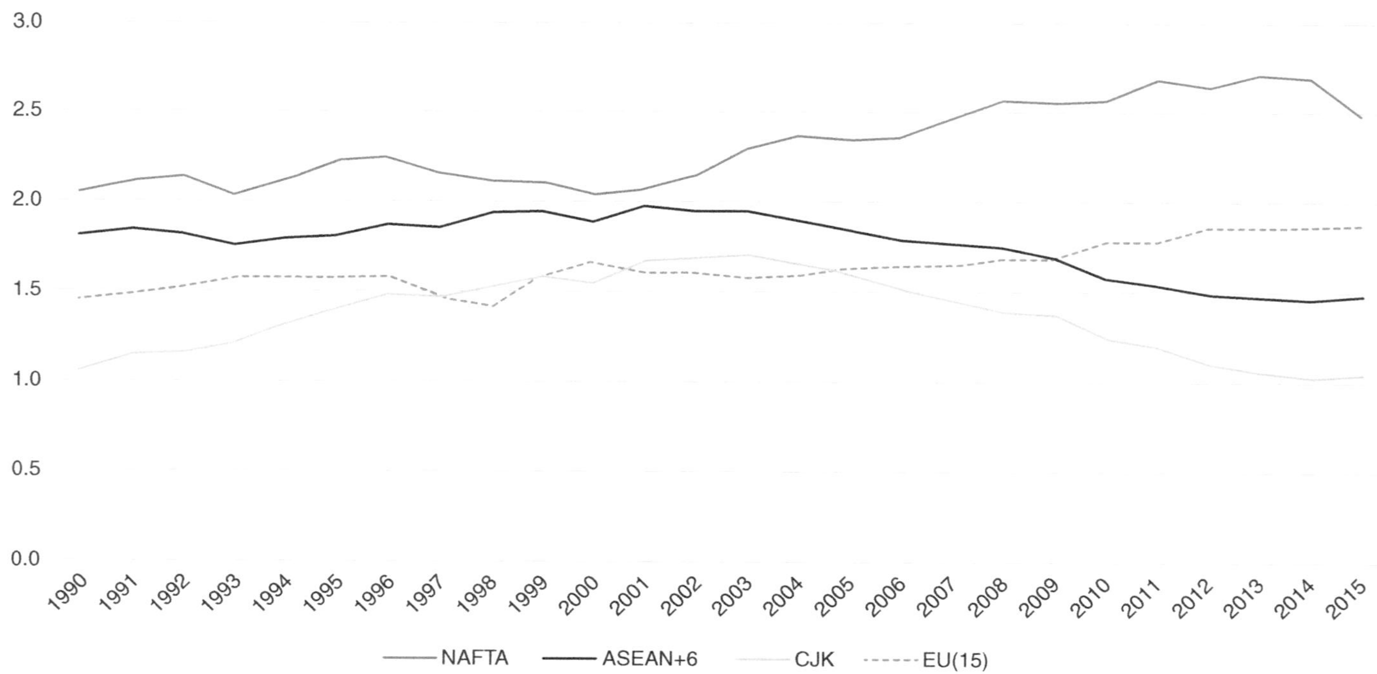

Figure 6.5 Simple concentration ratios of East Asia and other major economic regions

Source: Calculated from IMF (2015), DOTS Database (accessed on 30 June 2016).

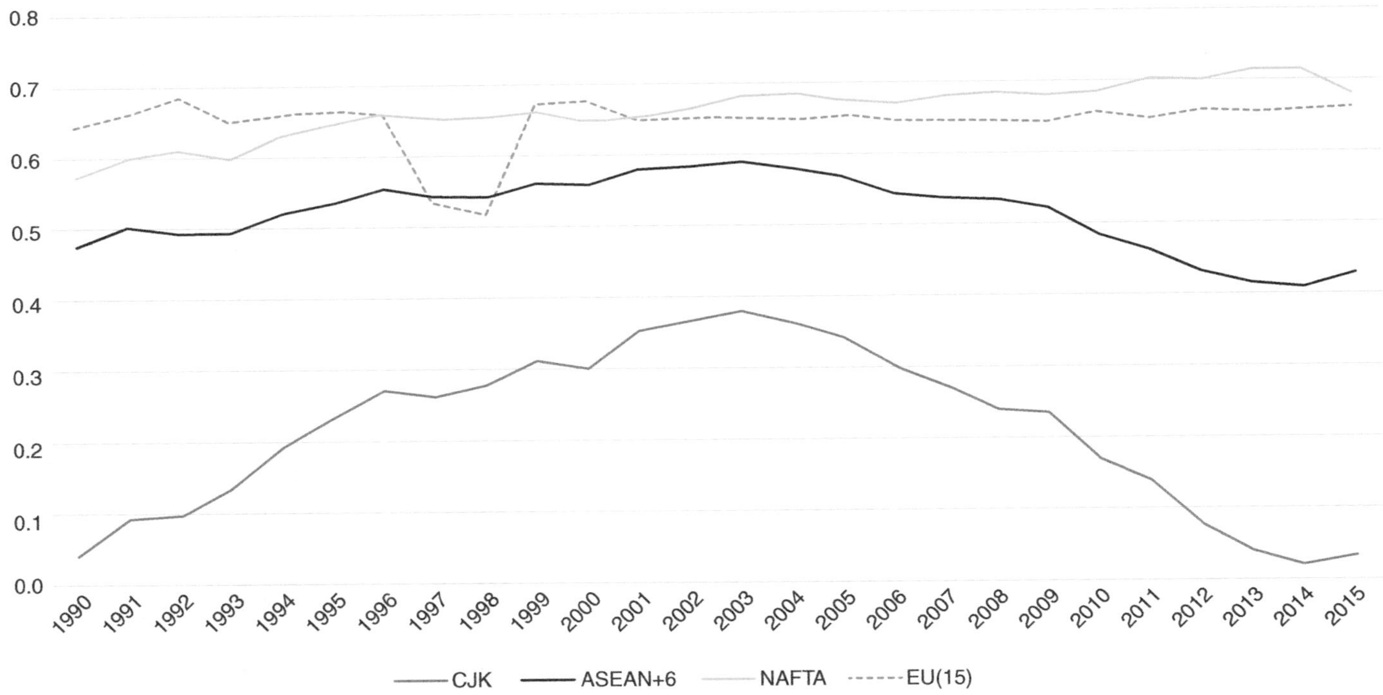

Figure 6.6 Regional introversion index of East Asia and other major economic regions

Source: Calculated from IMF (2015), DOTS Database (accessed on 30 June 2016).

Table 6.4 Trade dependencies of East Asian countries (%)

Country	*RCEP*		*ASEAN*		*CJK*	
	1990	*2015*	*1990*	*2015*	*1990*	*2015*
Brunei	78.0	28.2	25.7	10.3	50.7	13.4
Cambodia	74.8	63.0	59.2	39.0	12.5	22.8
Indonesia	59.6	58.5	9.9	22.5	45.2	28.5
Laos	89.4	97.4	65.3	68.4	23.3	27.1
Malaysia	53.2	50.4	24.0	22.1	25.0	22.8
Myanmar	44.6	93.7	18.3	36.5	21.7	51.3
Philippines	33.5	44.1	8.6	15.0	21.9	27.1
Singapore	49.7	67.5	22.6	32.2	23.1	30.0
Thailand	47.9	56.7	13.2	21.7	31.5	29.5
Vietnam	57.8	61.2	33.5	14.1	22.7	43.0
China	19.7	31.7	5.3	12.2	12.8	14.6
Japan	5.7	46.5	2.7	15.0	2.0	26.5
Korea	38.7	47.0	8.5	12.1	26.1	30.2
Australia	44.1	66.9	8.8	14.2	29.6	46.5
New Zealand	46.3	57.5	5.1	12.8	20.5	28.9
India	15.4	27.3	3.9	9.3	9.2	15.9
	China		*Japan*		*Korea*	
	1990	*2015*	*1990*	*2015*	*1990*	*2015*
Brunei	0.9	4.3	41.7	6.0	8.1	3.1
Cambodia	3.7	15.8	8.8	4.0	0.0	3.0
Indonesia	3.3	13.8	36.6	9.7	5.3	5.0
Laos	10.6	23.3	12.7	1.8	0.0	1.9
Malaysia	2.0	12.7	19.5	7.0	3.5	3.1
Myanmar	10.8	42.4	8.8	5.5	2.0	3.3
Philippines	1.1	10.4	17.6	11.0	3.2	5.7
Singapore	2.9	17.3	17.2	6.5	3.0	6.2
Thailand	2.6	15.0	26.3	11.9	2.7	2.6
Vietnam	0.5	25.2	19.2	7.3	3.0	10.5
China			12.3	7.3	0.5	7.2
Japan	0.8	21.0			1.2	5.5
Korea	0.0	23.0	26.1	7.2		
Australia	2.6	28.3	22.9	11.7	4.1	6.5
New Zealand	1.1	18.9	16.4	6.4	3.1	3.6
India	0.1	11.1	8.0	2.2	1.1	2.6

Source: Calculated from IMF (2015), DOTS Database (accessed on 30 June 2016).

a reversal in East Asian countries' trade dependency on Japan and China over the past twenty-five years. In 1990, the trade dependency on Japan for all East Asian countries except Myanmar was higher than that on China. However, in 2015, the trade dependency on China of all East Asian countries except Brunei and the Philippines was higher than that of Japan.

The dynamics between East Asian and Northeast Asian economic integration

East Asia has been, in many ways, the main arena for institutional economic integration over the past twenty-five years. The AFTA Agreement was signed among six ASEAN countries in 1992 and extended to all ten ASEAN countries by 1999. In addition, following the Asian financial crisis, the ASEAN+3 framework gradually evolved. Additionally, the East Asia Summit in which ASEAN, Australia, China, India, Japan, Korea and New Zealand participate, was established in December 2005, and the US and Russia have also become its members since November 2011.

Following the proposals of the EAVG and EASG, and based on the recommendations of the Joint Expert Group for Feasibility Study on EAFTA and the Track Two study on CEPEA, the process of forming a region-wide FTA in East Asia was launched. In November 2011, ASEAN took the initiative and proposed the ASEAN Framework for the Regional Comprehensive Economic Partnership (RCEP). The leaders of sixteen East Asian countries declared the start of RCEP negotiations in November 2012. Accordingly, the RCEP negotiations have been held since May 2013. Furthermore, the process of East Asian institutional economic integration was instrumental in initiating the process of Northeast Asian institutional economic integration. It was during the ASEAN+3 Summit held in Manila in November 1999 that the leaders of China, Japan and Korea had their first historic gathering, which became a formalized Trilateral Summit in 2002 before holding the Independent Trilateral Summit from December 2008.

A window of opportunity presented itself for the Northeast Asian countries to assume leadership in the regional economic integration process. Based on the trilateral joint research and the Joint Study Committee for a CJK FTA, the final decision to launch the CJK FTA was also made in November 2012. Subsequently, the first round of the CJK FTA negotiations took place in March 2013, followed by three other rounds of CJK FTA negotiations. The CJK FTA negotiations preceded those for the RCEP. Since the CJK FTA negotiations among three countries would appear to be much easier to conclude than RCEP negotiations involving sixteen countries, the CJK FTA negotiations may be concluded earlier than the RCEP negotiations if the three countries proceed in earnest; in so doing, they could then facilitate the RCEP negotiations.

The political relations among the three Northeast Asian countries deteriorated rapidly from the second half of 2012. As a result, the Sixth Trilateral Summit, which was supposed to be held in 2013, took place in November 2015, almost three and half years after the Fifth Summit in May 2012. Under these circumstances, the CJK FTA negotiations could not proceed properly, causing the CJK FTA negotiation process to lag behind that of the RCEP. Thus, the window of opportunity for Northeast Asia to catch up and surpass East Asia in terms of institutional economic influence and integration has somewhat closed.

Unlike the case of institutional economic integration, the interaction between Northeast Asian economic integration and East Asian economic integration in terms of functional economic integration cannot be clearly defined. Thus, as an alternative, one can assess the trend of the trade dependency of CJK on East Asia, on the one hand, and that of East Asian countries' trade dependency on CJK on the other. In this regard, the analyses indicate that the trade dependency of CJK on East Asia and that of East Asia on CJK generally has increased over the past twenty-five years. Positive inter-actions appear to have existed between functional economic integration in Northeast Asia and functional economic integration in East Asia.

Conclusion

The emergence of a Northeast Asian community and the nascent political and economic cooperation among CJK will require a strategic repositioning of other economic partners in the Asia-Pacific region, including the US, Australia and the EU, given that they have a strong economic interest in this region. As proposed in Chapter 1, the future trend of regional economic integration could be developed along two competing parallel trajectories: the first is the establishment of the China-led CJK economic cluster and incorporation of other groups later on, and the second is a US-led competing regional economic group through the promotion and strengthening of the formation of the bilateral trading blocs.

The development underpinning both trajectories could lead to a very different outcome in terms of geo-political and economic relationships in the Asia-Pacific region. Irrespective of the trajectories, however, trilateral economic integration (CJK FTA) and negotiations are likely to face a greater number of hurdles than solutions in coming years. Examples of the possible issues include the complicated geopolitics in Northeast Asia, such as North Korea's nuclear threat, and uncertain factors such as the worsening relationship between Korea and China due to Korea's recent (March 2017) deployment of the THAAD system in Korea against North Korea's latest nuclear and satellite tests.

While further development along the lines of CJK integration is possible, it is premature to expect that China, Japan and Korea's political and economic systems are soon to be more fully incorporated. This will certainly require joint political commitment from the governments of all three countries and the political leadership to realize the regional integration is the key development to ensure regional security, economic prosperity and political stability. An interdisciplinary approach combining three sectors, namely the state, society and the market, needs to be adopted in the Northeast Asian regional integration discussion (Ahn and Park 2007). While the motivation for the integration is based on economic calculations, the process of integration is clearly political. As was the case of European integration, coalition formation and leadership are now central aspects in the Northeast Asian integration (Laursen 2008: 5). While widening the membership of any agreement merely involves the extension of the cooperation to more actors, deepening it can be more complex and controversial and will depend on whether the individual CJK countries seek to expand economic ties or whether they would want to secure the political gains from closer integration and cooperation. As Hoffmann (1966) argued some years ago in the case of European Community (neo-functionalist view), "Every international system owes its inner logic and its unfolding to the diversity of domestic determinants, geo-historical situations and outside aims among its units" (Hoffmann 1966: 864). As such, strong and focused political leadership will be required for the success of those wanting more complex, multi-party negotiations in Asia.

Notes

1 East Asia Vision Group Report (2001). *Towards an East Asian Community, Region of Peace, Prosperity and Progress.*
2 *Final Report of the East Asia Study Group.* ASEAN+3 Summit, 4 November 2002, Phnom Penh.
3 "ASEAN Plus Three Cooperation, Joint Media Statement on the 18th AEM Plus Three Consultations", 23 August 2015, Kuala Lumpur.
4 The APTA was previously known as "the Bangkok Agreement" until it was renamed in November 2005. China joined in 2001.
5 Closer Economic Relations (CER), also known as the Australia-New Zealand Closer Economic Relations Trade Agreement (ANZCERTA) and sometimes shortened to CERTA, came into force on 1 January 1983, but the actual treaty was not signed until 28 March 1983.
6 ADB, Asia Regional Integration Centre (https://aric.adb.org/fta-country).
7 During the same period, the share of ASEAN+3 countries in the world's GDP rose from 17.8 per cent to 25.9 per cent (IMF. World Economic Outlook 2016 (accessed 3 June 2016)).
8 WTO, Statistics (accessed on June 5, 2016).
9 UNCTAD, Statistics (accessed on 20 June 2016).

7 Enhancing Northeast Asian integration

Introduction

This book has provided a detailed examination and analysis of the evolution and progress of Northeast Asian integration using geo-political, economic, historical, social and cultural perspectives. Several key themes and issues were discussed, and a series of questions and propositions were addressed. Four key themes and associate issues underpin the analysis.

First, the influence of geo-political power shifts and strategic challenges. These include the emergence of China in terms of political and economic strength through the 'One Belt and One Road' initiative, the US influence through the 'Asia-Pacific Rebalance Strategy' under the Obama administration and the 'Indo-Pacific Engagement Strategy' under the current Trump administration, the transformation of Japan under the Abe government with an emphasis on reforming the constitution and becoming a leader in the Asia-Pacific region; and the changes of leadership in South Korea and dealing with North Korea's nuclear threat as well as balancing the power between China and the US in the region.

Second, the economic rationale for promoting new regionalism. Such a rationale appears to focus on a 'building block' approach, that emphasizes developing rules and the trade-investment-service nexus with the complementary 'synergy of multilateralism' towards free trade, rather than 'a stumbling block' approach that would focus on tariff reduction among members with an intention to form an exclusive zone. Given that China has transformed rapidly in economic terms, with a corresponding increase in the number of people in the middle class, coupled with the growing capability of industry and services, it would appear almost a given that a more closely integrated regional economy would benefit CJK as well as other Asian countries.

Third, a number of historical factors remain key barriers for building trust relationships among three key CJK countries. It appears that these past animosities and competing claims are not able to be put to one side and that they have taken on the role of pre-conditions for the establishment of an integrated regional economy. Nevertheless, these factors have not prevented private sector trade arrangements from taking place, but it has meant that institutional building has been slow in the region. By comparison with the EU integration, the process of Northeast Asian integration is rather slow and clearly problematic.

Finally, a variety of social and cultural factors can be seen both as positive and negative drivers of regional integration. The CJK countries share similar roots of civilization, such as Confucianism, Buddhism and written languages. The cultural closeness enhances people-to-people exchanges and better mutual understanding. The social norms of reciprocity, fidelity, social network building, social hierarchy and collectivism can be considered as common norms among the people of CJK. Such common norms ease the relationship building at the individual level as well as at the level of business engagement and the country negotiation process among the CJK.

These common phenomena, however, can also be used for criticism if one party does not fulfil certain obligations for other parties. This was clearly the case in the Chinese and Korean leaders' criticisms of the Japanese government's lack of remorse and sincerity regarding the Japanese invasion and occupation in the twentieth century, and the associated issue of the so-called 'comfort women'. On the other hand, the Japanese leadership thought that the Chinese and Korean leaders were jeopardizing further regional cooperation by being unable to put aside historical problems.

Using these key themes and issues as a basis to our analysis has allowed us to see how regional integration could be enhanced or jeopardized by numerous factors, with many of these factors being non-economic in nature. Consequently, economic factors, which are generally supportive of regional integration, may well be relegated to a less significant role in any discussion on a CJK FTA by political leaders. This book therefore contributes to the social political literature on regional integration and extends the analysis beyond the economic domain. By doing so, this book allows us to address the questions and propositions presented in Chapter 1 in a more complete and holistic way.

Questions

Five key questions were posed at the beginning of this book. A brief summary of the responses to the questions is presented in Table 7.1. Question 1 asks about the current state of play, how well advanced the plans are for regional integration between CJK, and whether it can continue to work in the future. This question is important as it addresses the intent of the parties and whether they see the economic and political advantages of regional integration. Chapter 4 addressed this question in some detail. Since the launch of the CJK FTA negotiations in November 2012 in Phnom Penh, ongoing negotiations among the three countries have occurred, although they have not resulted in an agreed outcome. A total of thirteen rounds of negotiations have been conducted with the last round being held in Seoul in March 2018 where trade in goods, trade in services and investment were the key issues under discussion. However, during the process of negotiations, some agreements have been achieved, including a trilateral investment agreement in 2014 (Tiezzi 2014). This is an agreement that

Table 7.1 Research questions and responses

No.	*Questions*	*Responses*
1	What is the current state of play of the CJK FTA negotiations?	• Negotiations launched in 2012 and commenced in 2013. • A total of thirteen rounds of negotiations up to March 2018. • CJK countries committed to continue to work towards a CJK FTA.
2	Who benefits from a CJK FTA?	• China gains more political influence over the geo-political competition with the US. • Japan and Korea gain significant economic benefits.
3	What factors will influence the shape and level of economic integration?	• Critical factors are non-economic issues. • The role of the US. • CJK self-protection important and integration into the wider Asian region.
4	How will CJK leadership change influence the progress of the CJK FTA?	• 2013 leadership change cordial but uneven. • Little improvement until 2017. • Resumed talks in 2017 productive.
5	What are the critical issues and challenges for the realization of a CJK FTA?	• Common views: economic benefits for the three countries, spill over to other Asian economies. • Different views (China): CJK FTA a useful platform for regional integration (RCEP or ASEAN+3). • Different views (Japan and Korea): want to establish a high-level and high-standard FTA with detailed regulations and governing structures.

will clearly assist in advancing the integration of Asia's north eastern economies. Although the negotiations for a FTA have been slow, they will continue towards finality as clear economic advantages exist in the three countries building closer economic ties. This appears to be recognized by the three countries who have stated their commitment to continue to work towards this objective.

Question 2 considers who will benefit most among CJK countries from this new form of economic integration, and the political and economic gains. The evidence gathered for this book demonstrates that all three countries will benefit from a CJK FTA. For China, political gain appears to be the most important factor in the FTA given the geo-political competition with the US. Any leverage that will arise from regional integration among the CJK, where the other two countries are traditional allies of the US, would enhance the power and influence of China in the region. For Japan and Korea, the large Chinese domestic market in China provides significant economic benefit for both countries due to the growing middle class.

The increasing integration of production and supply chains among manufacturing industries in the three countries could be further enhanced by a CJK FTA with more rationalization among the key stakeholders dealing with supply, production and distribution in the region. As such, the services sector will also benefit from closer economic integration, whether it is related to tourism and hospitality, trade services, or financial services and professional services, such as accounting and legal services. Eventually, people- – to-people exchange activities will be more frequent and that will include students gaining part of their education in one of the other two countries. These exchanges will feed into the human resource needs for future cooperation among the three countries.

The third question asks about how the uncertain prospects for stability in Northeast Asia due to historical and cultural animosities and differences in political, social and historical perspectives will influence the shape and level of economic integration. The evidence collected shows that the critical barriers are non-economic factors, and include fundamental differences in political systems, current territorial and historical disputes, and a lack of community consciousness (Choi 2013: 105). Influence from external powers may also become key obstacles, such as the influence of the US over decisions made by the governments of Japan and South Korea.

In order to overcome these barriers and difficulties, the leadership of the three countries will have to lead with good will and focus on building trust relationships among themselves first. The current geo-political and economic tensions in the region, such as the US withdrawal from the TPP and talk of protectionism (Solis 2017; Donnelly 2018), could well increase the incentives for further integration among the CJK countries to protect their trade interests. It may well be that the formation of the CJK FTA is an inevitable result, and it remains only a matter of when and how.

Question 4 raises the issue of the influence of the changing leadership in CJK on the progress of CJK FTA negotiations. A change in CJK leadership occurred in 2013 when President Xi in China, President Park in South Korea and Prime Minister Abe in Japan rose to power. The relationships among them were cordial but uneven with a much closer relationship between Xi and Park, compared to that between Xi and Abe or between Park and Abe. However, the increasing tension caused by North Korea's nuclear ambitions, coupled with the subsequent push by the US for the deployment of the THAAD missile defence system led to a deterioration in the relationship between Xi and Park.

The economic relationship was also affected by the Chinese government's scrutiny of South Korean business' operating in China as well as blocking Chinese tourists visiting South Korea (Padden 2017). Due to the territorial disputes and historical issues among the CJK countries, the relationships between Xi and Abe as well as Park and Abe did not really improve until 2017 when Japan adopted much a warmer approach towards China and South Korean's newly elected President Moon eased the tensions between China and South Korea. Further engagement and productive negotiations among the CJK resumed and more positive outcomes were reached during the thirteenth round of negotiations in March 2018.

The final question, Question 5, raised the issue of the critical issues and challenges for the realization of the CJK economic clustering. There are common as well as different views among the Chinese, Japanese and Koreans on this question. The common goal is to extend economic benefits for the three countries beyond those which currently exist, which will eventually spill over to other Asian economies. Moreover, the economic complementarity between CJK countries will also lead to improved outcomes.

Each of the CJK countries also has different perspectives on the critical issues and challenges. From a Chinese perspective, a CJK FTA is a useful platform for regional integration and could fit into a larger Asian picture with a more ambitious regional integration objective such as the RCEP or ASEAN+3. As the largest economy in this grouping, and without strong US connections, China could play a much more pivotal leadership role. Therefore, for China a quick deal without too much detail on regulations and governing architecture within the treaty would probably be in its best interests. Details could be developed over time once the FTA is in place with other rules being added on a needs basis. On the other hand, Japan and South Korea would prefer to establish a high-level and high-standard FTA with all the detailed regulations and governing structures agreed to before implementation. Both countries are concerned about a lack of detailed rules and regulations at the beginning as they perceive a powerful nation such as China could change or introduce key provisions according to its needs at a later stage, thus leaving the other countries more vulnerable and with less economic power. The eventual outcome would be a compromise, but it probably would require China to provide more concessions in the negotiations, and work with Japan and Korea on developing more detailed rules and standards before finally reaching the agreement of CJK FTA.

Propositions

In the introductory chapter, we highlighted seven propositions related to the key issues underpinning this book. We now address these propositions based on the findings presented in previous chapters. A brief summary of the responses to the propositions is presented in Table 7.2.

> **Proposition 1**: Despite the significant implications of economic and political arrangements in Northeast Asia and the pressure for change and advancement, much of the literature on economic integration (i.e. FTAs) seems to be within the field of economics focusing on the welfare implications of FTAs, both for members and the world.

This proposition reflects current research on FTAs based on economics with a focus on economic benefits for member countries and the world. Other factors and implications, such as geo-political issues, historical challenges and social/

Table 7.2 Propositions and responses

No.	*Key Propositions*	*Responses*
1	Much of the literature on economic integration is within the field of economics focusing on the welfare implications of FTAs.	• Strong support for proposition. • Other factors such as geo-political issues, historical challenges and social/cultural norms are neglected.
2	CJK's progress on regionalism is not simply a calculation based on economic optimality.	• Strong support for proposition. • Other factors included historical background, changes in domestic political and economic systems and social/cultural norms.
3	Economic benefits as well as strong political and economic pressures motivate each country to establish a CJK FTA.	• Support for proposition. • Many uncertainties in the region. • Economically and politically a CJK FTA could be seen as a positive initiative.
4	Resumption of the CJK FTA talks in recent years is the response to the rapidly changing internal and external political economy environment.	• Strong support for proposition. • These factors suggest that China may need to make more concessions to Japan and Korea in order to gain more support.
5	The TPP and RCEP may lead to a new form of geo-political power game between the US, China and Japan.	• Proposition no longer applicable. • US withdrawal from the TPP has led to a repositioning of actors. • This could lead to a speed up the CJK FTA negotiations.
6	The US, China and Japan will each try to shape economic groupings in the region to promote their respective interests.	• Strong support for proposition. • CJK countries will take a strategic approach to the formation of regional groupings. • Recognition that CJK are economically interdependent.
7	China's approach to the new Asian regionalism (AIIB, RCEP, FTAAP) reduces the influence of the US's TPP.	• Weak support for proposition. • China will do everything it can to protect its regional interests. • The CJK and other regional groupings will form a significant part of their strategy. • Uncertain role for the US at present.

cultural norms have generally been overlooked by the mainstream literature in the field of economics on FTAs. Where such factors have been considered, only passing mention has been made of the difficulties such factors present.

Proposition 2: CJK's active progress on regionalism is the response to the rapidly changing political economy of Northeast Asia rather than a simple calculation based on economic optimality.

The evidence provided in previous chapters supports this proposition. Based on their historical background, the three countries have changed dramatically with the significant geo-political power shift, the changes in domestic political and economic systems and social/cultural norms. These factors certainly require more consideration when attempting to understand what has influenced CJK's progress on regionalism.

> **Proposition 3**: While Northeast Asian economic cooperation has only been sporadically achieved and its future remains uncertain, there are not only economic benefits from the realization of the CJK FTA, but also strong political and economic pressures and expectations that motivate each nation to push for the CJK FTA.

This proposition is supported. The social, political and economic uncertainty in Asia, particularly after the Trump administration assumed power in the US and the associated increasing tensions in the areas of regional security and trade, are likely to leave the three countries in the Northeast Asia region feeling vulnerable and the need for more cohesive integration. Moving forward to establish a CJK FTA could be seen as a positive initiative for building a mutual support platform in the region.

> **Proposition 4**: Resumption of the CJK FTA talks in recent years is a response to the rapidly changing internal and external political-economic environment rather than a simple calculation based on economic optimality. As such, this move towards regionalism presents a wide range of economic and political challenges and opportunities for neighbouring countries.

Once again, this proposition is supported by the evidence provided in previous chapters. The action taken by the US to withdraw from the TPP, as well as recent trade initiatives by the Trump administration (Stewart 2018) could trigger a global trade confrontation among the major players, in particular between China and the US. Therefore, it may be in China's best interests to provide some concessions to its neighbours, namely Japan and South Korea in order to gain more mutual support among CJK members. A CJK FTA will play an important role in this regard.

> **Proposition 5**: The TPP (Trans-Pacific Partnership) and RCEP (Regional Comprehensive Economic Partnership) (FTAAP – Free Trade Agreement of Asia-Pacific) may lead to a new form of geo-political power game between the US, China and Japan, which inevitably carries political and security implications.

Given the recent change in US policy on the TPP, this proposition is probably no longer applicable in its present form. Nevertheless, the remaining eleven TPP countries acted quickly to form a modified version of the TPP (the CPTPP) without US involvement (Sherwood and Iturrieta 2018). Although the US government has indicated that it might wish to join the TPP in the future under a different set of conditions, the other members have clearly indicated that no more negotiations would take place with the US around the current stipulated agreement. Therefore, the US rejoining the TPP (or CPTTP) will not happen quickly nor is it a foregone conclusion, although improved access to the large US market is certainly an attraction for the CPTTP countries. Moreover, as mentioned earlier, one consequence of the US withdrawal from the TPP is that it could lead to a stronger desire by CJK countries to conclude the CJK FTA negotiations.

> **Proposition 6**: Each country will be trying to shape economic cooperation groupings in Southeast and Northeast Asia and in the wider Asia-Pacific region to promote its respective economic interests. This may have unpredictable, unproductive and even dangerous political consequences for the CJK FTA or Northeast Asian economic integration in the near future.

This proposition is supported. Although the major players, including CJK countries, will develop their own strategic positions and options with other partners in the region, fundamentally CJK countries need each other to gain the required economic (and political) integration. The process of formation of the CJK FTA will take time and effort, but the eventual outcome will be reached assuming the political will exists among the three participants. It is hard to predict whether there would be adverse political consequences in this regard.

> **Proposition 7**: China's progressive approach to the new Asian regionalism (i.e. AIIB – Asian Infrastructure Investment Bank, RCEP and FTAAP) reduces the influence of the US's preferred Asian regional architecture (i.e. the TPP). The TPP (or similar arrangements) will be a major challenge to China's ambition to achieve a Peaceful Rise.

There is some support for this proposition. Given China is facing a serious challenge from the US-led 'Indo-Pacific Strategy', China will do everything possible to protect its interests in the region. By working together with other regional countries through the formation of the CJK FTA, and eventually the formation of the RCEP, China could play a critical role in moving forward the regional economic integration agenda without US involvement. On the other hand, given that the US has withdrawn from the TPP and has not indicated that it will attempt to open discussions or rejoin it in the near future, the immediate challenge from the TPP has not materialized. There have also been discussions about China joining the newly formed CPTPP in the near future. This could play out as one of the proactive contributions of China to the different forms of regional trade architecture.

Conclusion

The first round of CJK FTA negotiations took place in Seoul, Korea in March 2013 and as of March 2018, thirteen rounds of FTA negotiations have been held. Whilst agreement has yet to be reached, some progress has been made and the parties have agreed that "one common schedule should be the main means of the CJK FTA commitments, while the possibility of bilateral schedules could be explored to achieve a higher level of liberalization" (Lee 2015: 34). No consensus on trade in services liberalization methods has been reached but the parties have agreed to adopt a negative list approach and that some progress has been made on intellectual property rights, competition policy, rules of origin (ROO), SPS and TBT.

To realize the Era of East Asia, East Asia countries will need to maintain the region's economic growth, enlarge internal domestic markets and create a stable international political and security environment. To satisfy these conditions, a region-wide FTA is probably the best way to proceed. If this is the case, then the most fundamental task for achieving this objective is the formation of a FTA among China, Japan and South Korea. This agreement is by no means assured and this book has highlighted the factors influencing the process of negotiation to date, the key drivers of this process and the very real barriers to achieving a CJK FTA.

The Northeast Asian community and the nascent political and economic cooperation among CJK countries will also require a strategic repositioning of other economic partners in the Asia-Pacific region, including the US, Australia and the EU, given they have a strong economic interest in this region. To achieve such an outcome will require the state, society and markets to be integrated into the Northeast Asian regional integration discussions (Ahn and Park 2007). While the motivation for the integration is based on economic calculations, the process of integration is clearly social and political. As was the case with European integration, coalition formation and leadership are now central aspects in the Northeast Asian integration process (Laursen 2008: 5). While widening the membership of any agreement involves the extension of the cooperation to more actors, deepening it can be more complex and controversial, and will depend on whether the individual CJK countries seek to expand economic ties or whether they would want to secure the political gains from closer integration and cooperation.

Bibliography

Ahn, C. Y. and Cheong, I. K. (2007). 'A Search for Closer Economic Relations in East Asia', *The Japanese Economic Review*, 58(2): 173–190.

Ahn, C. Y. and Jung, S. C. (2012). *Korea-Japan Economic Cooperation amid a New East Asian Integration with an Emphasis on FDI Flows*, Seoul: Korea Institute for International Economic Policy (KIEP).

Ahn, H. D. (2006). 'FTA Policies of CJK and Prospects of CJK FTA: Korean Perspective', Paper presented at the International Conference on "Prospects for Regional FTA(s) in Northeast Asia" organized by Korea Institute for International Economic Policy (KIEP) in Seoul, Korea, 14 December, 2006.

Ahn, H. and Park, J. (2007). *A Political-Economic Approach to Northeast Asian Regional Cooperation: Search for a New Model and Korea's Strategies* (in Korean), Seoul: Korea Institute for Industrial Economics and Trade.

Aminian, N. (2005). 'Economic Integration and Prospects for Regional Monetary Cooperation in East Asia', *Structural Change and Economic Dynamics*, 16(1): 91–110.

Andriamananjara, S. (2011). 'Customs Union', in Chauffour Jean-Pierre, Jean-Christophe Maur (eds.), *Preferential Trade Agreement Policies for Development: A Handbook*, Chapter 5,Washington, DC: The World Bank, pp. 111–120.

ASEAN (2015). 'ASEAN Plus Three Cooperation, Joint Media Statement on the 18th AEM Plus Three Consultations', 23 August, 2015, Kuala Lumpur.

Asia Regional Integration Centre (2017). https://aric.adb.org/fta-country. [accessed on 13 December 2017].

Baier, S. L., Bergstrand, J. H. and Egger, P. (2006). 'The New Regionalism: Causes and Consequences', paper rewritten for the Inter-American Development and CEPII Conference, February 9–10.

Bailey, K. (1987). *Methods of Social Research*, New York: The Free Press.

Balassa, B. (1967). 'Trade Creation and Trade Diversion in the European Common Market', *Economic Journal*, 77(305): 1–21.

Baldwin, R. E. (1995). 'The Domino Theory of Regionalism', in R. Baldwin, P. Haaparanta. and J. Kiander (eds.), *Expanding membership of the European Union*, Cambridge: Cambridge University Press.

Baldwin, R. E. (2006). 'Multilateralising Regionalism: Spaghetti Bowls as Building Blocs on the Path to Global Free Trade', *The World Economy*, 29(11): 1451–1518.

Baldwin, R. E. (2008). *The Development and Testing of Heckscher-Ohlin Trade Models: A Review*, Cambridge, MA: MIT Press.

Baldwin, R. E. (2011).'21st Century Regionalism: Filling the Gap between 21st Century Trade and 20th Century Trade Rules', *World Trade Organization, Staff Working Paper ERSD-2011–08*, Geneva: World Trade Organization.

Baldwin, R. E. and Carpenter, T. (2009).'A 3 Bloc Dance: East Asian Regionalism and the North Atlantic Trade Giants', Gateway, www.sussex.ac.uk/webteam/gateway/file.php?name=5.pdf&site=261 [accessed on 27 August 2017].

Baldwin, R. E. and Freund, C. (2011). 'Preferential Trade Agreements and Multilateral Liberalization', in Chauffour Jean-Pierre, Jean-Christophe Maur (eds.), *Preferential Trade Agreement Policies for Development: A Handbook*, Chapter 6, pp. 121–142, Washington D.C.: World Bank.

Bergsten, F. (1996a).'Globalizing Free Trade: The Ascent of Regionalism', *Foreign Affairs*, 75(3) May/June: 105–120.

Bergsten, F. (1996b).'Competitive Liberalization and Global Free Trade: A Vision for the Early 21st Century', *Working Paper 96–15*, Washington D.C.: Peterson Institute for International Economics.

Bloomberg (2013). 'After Japan Joins Talks, China Considering TPP', The Japan Times, 01 June 2013, www.japantimes.co.jp/news/2013/06/01/business/after-japan-joins-talks-china-considering-tpp/#.WriL2dIUn48 [accessed on 01/06/2017].

Buckley, P. J. and Casson, M. (1976). *The Future of the Multinational Enterprise*, London: MacMillan.

Burfisher, M., Robinson, S. and Thierfelder, K. (2004). 'Regionalism: Old and New Theory and Practice', *MTID Discussion Paper*, No.65, Washington, DC: International Food Policy Research Institute.

Cai, K. G. (2010). *The Politics of Regionalism: Explaining Regional Economic Integration in East Asia*, New York: Palgrave Macmillan.

CEIC (2015). 'China Premium Database' (www.ceicdata.com/en/country/china) [accessed on 15 June 2016].

Chen, L. X. and Wang, F. (2017). 'Japan's Abe Signals Support for China's 'Belt and Road' Initiative', *Caixin English*, 06 June 2017. www.caixinglobal.com/2017-06-06/101098774.html [accessed on 14 January 2018].

Cheong, I. (2003). 'Regional Economic Integration in Northeast Asia: Present and Future', Paper presented at the 4th China FTA Network. (2017). 12th Round of Negotiation of China-Japan-South Korea FTA Held in Tokyo Japan, 17 April 2017. http://fta.mofcom.gov.cn/enarticle/chinarihen/chinarihennews/201704/34740_1.html [accessed on 14 January 2018].

Cheong, I. (2005). 'Evaluation of Recent Progress of FTAs in East Asia – A Korean Perspective', in C. Y. Ahn et al. (eds.), *East Asian Economic Regionalism*, Netherlands: Springer, pp. 37–56.

Chia, S. Y. (2010). 'Regional Trade Policy Cooperation and Architecture in East Asia', *ADBI Working Paper*, No.191, Tokyo: Asian Development Bank Institute.

Choi, Y. M. (2013). 'Political Economy of Free Trade Agreements in China, Japan, and South Korea: Sectoral and National Security Politics of the FTA Wave', *Theses and Dissertations Paper*, No. 244, Milwaukee: University of Wisconsin–Milwaukee.

Crotty, J. and Lee, K. (2001). 'Economic Performance in Post-Crisis Korea: A Critical Perspective on Neoliberal Restructuring', *Seoul Journal of Economics*, 14(2): 183–242.

Davis, D. R. (1995). 'Intra-Industry Trade: A Heckscher-Ohlin-Ricardo Approach', *Journal of International Economics*, 39: 201–226.

De, P. (2006). 'Regional Trade in Northeast Asia: Why Do Trade Costs Matter?' *Cesifo Working Paper*, No.1809, Munich: Cesifo Group.

De, S. H. (2005). 'The Dragon and the Tigers: China and Asian Regionalism', *World Policy Journal*, 22(2): 23–36.

Department of Foreign Affairs and Trade (DFAT) (2015). Australia's trade and economic statistics in 2014. http://dfat.gov.au/about-us/publications/trade-investment/trade-at-a-glance/trade-at-a-glance-2015/Pages/australias-trade-and-economic-statistics-in-2014.aspx [accessed on 19 January 2018].

Delgado, M., Porter, M. and Stern, S. (2011). 'Clusters, Convergence, and Economic Performance', Astro Temple, 22 March 2011, http://astro.temple.edu/~mdelgado/index_files/DPS_Clusters_Performance_final_03_11_2011.pdf [accessed on 27 August 2017].

Donnelly, G. (2018). 'How Donald Trump's Steel and Aluminum Tariffs Could Start a Trade War', Fortune, 2 March 2018. http://fortune.com/2018/03/02/donald-trump-steel-aluminum-tariffs/ [accessed on 5 March 2018].

DRC/NIRA/KIEP (2004). 'Joint Report and Policy Recommendations on Sectoral Implications of a China-Japan-Korea FTA', The Development Research Center of China, National Institute for Research Advancement of Japan, and the Korea Institute for International Economic Policy, November 2004.

DRC/NIRA/KIEP (2011). 'Joint Study Report for an FTA among China, Japan and Korea', The Development Research Center of China, National Institute for Research Advancement of Japan, and the Korea Institute for International Economic Policy, 16 December 2011.

Dunning, J. (1988a). *Explaining International Production*, London: Routledge.

Dunning, J. (1988b). 'The Eclectic Paradigm of International Production: A Restatement and Some Possible Extensions', *Journal of International Business Studies*, 19: 1–31.

Dunning, J. (1995). 'Reappraising the Eclectic Paradigm in an Age of Alliance Capitalism', *Journal of International Business Studies*, 26(3): 461–493.

East Asia Study Group (EASG) (2002). *Final Report of the East Asia Study Group. ASEAN+3 Summit*, Phnom Penh, Cambodia: EASG.

East Asia Vision Group Report. (2001). *Towards an East Asian Community, Region of Peace, Prosperity and Progress*, Phnom Penh, Cambodia. Economics Online: www.economicsonline.co.uk/Global_economics/Customs_unions.html [accessed on 21 March 2018].

The Edge Financial Daily (2018). 'TPP and CPTPP: The differences and what it means for New Zealand', 26 January, p. 17.

Egger, P. (2006). 'The New Regionalism: Causes and Consequences', *paper rewritten for the Inter-American Development and CEPII Conference*, February 9–10.

Estrada, G., Park, D., Park, I. and Park, S. (2011). 'ASEAN's Free Trade Agreements with the People's Republic of China, Japan, and the Republic of Korea: A Qualitative and Quantitative Analysis', *Working Papers on Regional Economic Integration 75*, Manila: Asian Development Bank.

The Export and Import Bank of Korea, Outward FDI statistics: www.koreaexim.go.kr/site/main/index001online. [accessed on 15 June 2016].

Francois, J. F. and Wignaraja, G. (2008). 'Economic Implications of Asian Integration', *Global Economy Journal*, 8(3): 1–46.

Frankel, J. A. (1997). *Regional Trading Blocs in the World Economic System*, New York: Columbia University Press.

Gao, C. (2017). 'Was Moon Jae-in's China Trip Successful?' *The Diplomat*, 19 December 2017. http://thediplomat.com/2017/12/was-moon-jae-ins-china-trip-successful/ [accessed on 14 January 2018].

Gao, H. (2011). 'China's Strategy for Free Trade Agreements: Political Battle in the Name of Trade', in R. P. Buckley, R. W. Hu and D. W. Arner (eds.), *East Asia Economic Integration: Law, Trade and Finance*, London: Edward Elgar, pp. 104–120.

Gao, S. Q. (2000). 'Economic Globalization: Trends, Risks and Risk Prevention', *CDP Background Paper*, No. 1, New York: United Nations.

Gilpin, R. (1987). *The Political Economy of International Relations*, Princeton: Princeton University Press.

Glaser, B. and Strauss, A. (1967). *The Discovery of Grounded Theory: Strategies for Qualitative Research*, Chicago: Aldine.

Graham, E. and Krugman, P. (1979). 'Economic Impact', in E. Graham and P. Krugman (eds.), *Foreign Direct Investment in the United States*, Washington DC: Institute for International Economics, pp. 57–84.

Greenberg, J. D. (2015). 'The Elusive China-Japan-South Korea Free Trade Agreement', *MA Dissertation*, Monterey, CA: Naval Postgraduate School.

Griffith, M. K., Steinberg, R. and Zysman, J. (2015). 'Great Power Politics in a Global Economy: Origins and Consequences of the TPP and TTIP', presented at the Conference, 'Unpacking the Transatlantic Trade and Investment Partnership (TTIP) Negotiations' at Université Libre de Bruxelles (ULB), 17 October.

Hamanaka, S. (2012). 'Is Trade in Asia Really Integrating?' *ADB Working Paper Series on Regional Economic Integration*, Manila: Asian Development Bank.

Hamanaka, S. (2015). 'The Selection of Trade Integration Indicators: Intraregional Share, Intensity, Homogenous Intensity and Introversion Index', *ADB Economics Working Paper Series*, No.455, Manila: Asian Development Bank.

Hamanaka, Shintaro (2017). 'China-Japan-Korea Trilateral Investment Treaty: Implications for Future Investment Negotiation in Asia', in J. Chaisse, T. Ishikawa and S. Jusoh (eds.), *Asia's Changing International Investment Regime: Sustainability, Regionalization, & Arbitration*, Singapore: Springer, pp. 134–142.

Helpman E. and Krugman, P. R. (1985). *Market Structure and Foreign Trade*, Cambridge, MA: MIT Press.

Henderson, J. (1986), 'The New International Division of Labour and American Semiconductor Production in Southeast Asia', in C. Dixson, D. Drakakis-Smith and H. Watts (eds.), *Multinational Corporations and the Third World*, London: Croom Helm, pp. 91–117.

Hoffmann, S. (1966). 'Obstinate or Obsolete? The Fate of the Nation-State and the Case of Western Europe', *Daedalus*, 95(Summer): 862–915.

Hofmann, P. (2013). *The Impact of International Trade and FDI on Economic Growth and Technological Change, Contributions to Economics*, Verlag Berlin Heidelberg: Springer.

Holloway, J. (1994). 'Global Capital and the National State', *Capital and Class*, 52: 23–48.

Hosny, A. S. (2013). 'Theories of Economic Integration: A Survey of the Economic and Political Literature', *International Journal of Economy, Management and Social Sciences*, 2(5): 133–155.

Hymer, S. (1976). *The International Operations of National firms: A Study of Direct Foreign Investment*, Cambridge, MA: The MIT Press.

IMF (2015). Direction of Trade Statistics: http://data.imf.org/?sk=9D6028D4-F14A-464C-A2F2-59B2CD424B85 [accessed on 30 June 2016].

IMF (2016). World Economic Outlook Databases 2016: www.imf.org/external/pubs/ft/weo/2016/01/weodata/index.aspx [accessed on 3 June 2016].

International Monetary Fund (IMF) (1993). *Balance of Payments Manual*, 5th edition, Washington, DC: IMF.

The Japan Times. (2014). 'Record Number of Japanese Hostile toward China and South Korea: Cabinet Office Poll', *The Japan Times*, 20 December 2014.

The Japan Times. (2017). 'Japan and EU Hail Creation of a 'Gigantic Economic Zone' as Trade Talks Conclude', *The Japan Times*, 9 December 2017.

Jenkins, R. (1987). *Transnational Corporations and Uneven Development: The Internationalization of Capital and the Third World*, London: Methuen.

JETRO (2015). Japanese Trade and Investment Statistics www.jetro.go.jp/en/reports/statistics/ [accessed on 15 June 2016].

Jovanovic, M. (2006). *International Economic Integration: Limits and Prospects*, London: Routledge.

Kastner, S. (2011).'Does Economic Integration Augur Peace in East Asia?' *Current History*, September: 223–228.

Katada, S. N. (2009a). 'Political Economy of East Asian Regional Integration and Cooperation', *Asian Development Bank Institute (ADBI) Working Paper Series*, No.170, Tokyo: ADBE.

Katada, S. N. (2009b). 'Politics that Constrains: The Logic of Fragmented Regionalism in East Asia', *East Asia Institute (EAI) Working Paper*, No 21. October, Seoul: EAI.

Kawai, M. (2005). 'East Asian Economic Regionalism: Progress and Challenges', *Journal of Asian Economics*, 16: 29–55.

Kawai, M. and Wignaraja, G. (2010). 'Free Trade Agreements in East Asia: A Way toward Trade Liberalization?' *ADB Briefs*, June(1): 1–8.

Kawai, M. and Wignaraja, G. (2010a). 'Asian FTAs: Trends, Prospects and Challenges', *ADB Working Paper Series*, No.226, October, Manila: Asian Development Bank.

Keating, W. E. (2015). 'The Doha Round and Globalization: A Failure of World Economic Development?' City University of New York (CUNY) Academic Works. http://academicworks.cuny.edu/hc_sas_etds/7 [accessed on 28 December 2017].

Khanna, J. and Lee, C. J. (eds.) (1996). *Economic Interdependence and Challenges to the Nation-State Economic Cooperation in the Yellow Sea Rim*, Seoul: Korea Institute for International Economic Policy.

Kiely, R. (1994). 'Development Theory and Industrialization: Beyond the Impasse', *Journal of Contemporary Asia*, 24(2): 133–160.

Kiljunen, K. (1989). 'Toward A Theory of the International Division of Industrial Labour', *World Development*, 17(1): 109–138.

Kim, S. K. (2008). 'Theories and Realities of FTA Formation between Korea and Canada', *Korean Social Science Journal*, 35(2): 55–78.

Kim, T. W. and Hahm, H. E. (2018). 'Korea, China, Japan move ahead on free trade'. Korea.net (www.korea.net/NewsFocus/policies/view?articleId=156308) [accessed on 25 March 2018].

Koo, M. G. (2006). 'The Evolution and Implications of Bilateral Trade Agreements in the Asia-Pacific', in V. K. Aggarwal and S. Urata (eds.), *Bilateral Trade Agreements*

in the Asia-Pacific: Origins, Evolution, and Implications, London: Routledge, pp. 140–159.
Koo, M. G. (2010). 'Embracing Free Trade Agreements, Korean Style: From Developmental Mercantilism to Developmental Liberalism', *The Korean Journal of Policy Studies*, 25(3): 101–123.
Korea FTA Portal (2017) (www.customs.go.kr/kcshome/site/index.do;jsessionid=86PthJLbXSrWnhDBJdyFvGpThrw4LbqH2kCLrYh3yKnJFSwd4ZRy!130641230?layoutSiteId=ftaportalkor) [accessed on 27 February 2018].
The Korea Times. (2013). 'Japan's New Provocation', *The Korea Times*, Editorial, 23 February 2013.
Korean Ministry of Foreign Affairs and Trade (2013). www.mofat.go.kr/ENG/policy/fta/status/overview/index.jsp?menu=m_20_80_10 [accessed on February 2013].
Krueger, A. (1999). 'Are Preferential Trading Arrangements Trade-Liberalizing or Protectionist?' *The Journal of Economic Perspectives*, 13(4): 105–124.
Krugman, P. (1987). 'Is Free Trade Passé?' *Economic Perspectives*, 1(2): 131–144.
Laursen, F. (2008). 'Theory and Practice of Regional Integration', *The Jean Monnet/Robert Schuman Paper Series*, 8(3): 3–22.
Lawrence, R. Z. (1997). 'Preferential Trading Arrangements: The Traditional and the New', In A. Galal and B. Hoekman (eds.), *Regional Partners in Global Markets: Limits and Possibilities of the Euro-Med Agreements*, London: Center for Economic Policy Research, pp. 13–34.
Lee, C. J. (1996). 'Northeast Asian Economic Cooperation: An Olympic Model', *The Journal of Northern Area Economic Studies*, 7: 1–20. (in Korean).
Lee, C. J. (2015). 'Northeast Asian Economic Community: A Korean Perspective', in J. C. Lee and C. J. Lee (eds.), *Building a Northeast Asian Economic Community*, Sejong-Si: Korea Institute for International Economic Policy, pp. 25–38.
Lee, C. J. and Bang, H. K. (2011). *From Northeast Asian Economic Cooperation to East Asian Economic Integration: Toward an Era of East Asia (in Korean)*, Seoul: KIEP.
Lee, C. J., H. K. Bang, S. K. Na, and B. Lee (2012). *Trilateral Economic Cooperation: Proposal for Enhancing Economic Cooperation Dialogue Channels among China, Japan, and Korea*, Seoul: Korea Institute for International Economic Policy (in Korean).
Lee, E. J (2013). 'Abe Elevates Dokdo Unit in His Cabinet Secretariat', *Korea Choong-Ang Daily (English)*, February 9.
Lee, J. (2011). 'Senkaku/Diaoyu: Islands of Conflict', *History Today*, www.historytoday.com/archive/historytoday/2011/volume-61-issue-5 [accessed on 17 December 2017].
Lee, M. and Y, Oh (2012). *Road Map Toward the Era of Northeast Asia (in Korean)*, Seoul: Korea Institute for Industrial Economics and Trade (KIET).
Lee, T. H. (2016). '*One Belt, One Road Strategy and Korean-Chinese Cooperation. International Institute for Asian Studies*', the Newsletter, 74 Summer 2016.
Lee Y. I., Benson, J. and Zhu, Y. (2015). 'Economic Clustering in Northeast Asia: China, Japan, and Korea Integration', in A. P. D'Costa (ed.), *After-Development Dynamics: South Korea's Contemporary Engagement with Asia*, Oxford: Oxford University Press, pp. 29–44.
Levy, P. I. (1997). 'A Political-Economic Analysis of Free-Trade Agreements', *The American Economic Review*, 87(4): 506–519.

Lindberg, L. N. (1963). *The Political Dynamics of European Economic Integration*, Stanford: Stanford University Press.

Lipsey, R. G. (1957). 'The Theory of Customs Unions: Trade Diversion and Welfare', *Economica, New Series*, 24(February): 40–46.

Lipsey, R. G. (1960). 'The Theory of Customs Unions: A General Survey', *The Economic Journal*, 70(279): 498–513.

MacIntyre, R. (1990). 'The Political Economy and Class Analytics of International Capital Flows: United States Industrial Capital in the 1970s and 1980s', *Review of Radical Political Economics*, 22(1): 135–154.

Mansfield, E. and Milner, H. (1999). 'The New Wave of Regionalism', *International Organization*, 53(3): 589–627.

METI (2007). *Japan's EPA/FTA Policy*, Tokyo: Ministry of Economy, Trade and Industry.

MFAJ (2011). 'Joint Study Report for an FTA among China, Japan and Korea', Ministry of Foreign Affairs of Japan, 16 December 2011, www.mofa.go.jp/mofaj/press/release/24/3/pdfs/0330_10_01.pdf [accessed on 31 January 2018].

MFAJ (2017). 'Japan-China-Republic of Korea Free Trade Agreement', Ministry of Foreign Affairs of Japan, 7 April 2017, www.mofa.go.jp/ecm/ep/page23e_000337.html [accessed on 12 January 2018].

Ministry of Foreign Affairs of Japan (2018). Free Trade Agreement and Economic Partnership Agreement www.mofa.go.jp/policy/economy/fta/index.html [accessed on 22 March 2018].

Ministry of Foreign Affairs and Trade of Japan (MOFAT, Japan) (2012). 'Joint Declaration on the Enhancement of Trilateral Comprehensive Cooperative Partnership', the Fifth Trilateral Summit among the People's Republic of China, the Republic of Korea and Japan, 13 May 2012, Beijing. (www.mofa.go.jp/region/asia-paci/jck/summit1205/joint_declaration_en.html) [accessed].

Ministry of Foreign Affairs and Trade of Japan (MOFAT, Japan) (2015). "Joint Declaration for Peace and Cooperation in Northeast Asia, the Sixth Trilateral Summit among the People's Republic of China, the Republic of Korea and Japan, 1 November 2015, Seoul." (www.mofa.go.jp/a_o/rp/page1e_000058.html) [accessed].

Ministry of Commerce of the People's Republic of China, China FTA Network: (http://fta.mofcom.gov.cn/english/index.shtml) [accessed on 10 March 2018].

Ministry of Foreign Affairs and Trade of Republic of Korea (MOFAT, Korea). (2011). *Joint Study Report for an FTA among China, Japan and Korea*, Seoul: MOFAT.

Ministry of Trade, Industry and Energy of Republic of Korea: (http://fta.go.kr/main/situation/kfta/ov/) [accessed on 5 June 2016].

Ministry of Trade, Industry and Energy, Republic of Korea, FDI statistics www.motie.go.kr/motie/py/sa/investstatse/investstats.jsp [accessed on 15 June 2016].

Moran, R. E. and Katsikeas, C. S. (1997). 'Theories of International Trade, Foreign Direct Investment and Firm Internationalization: A Critique', *Management Decision*, 35(1): 68–78.

Munakata, N. (2002). 'Whither East Asian Economic Integration?' The Research Institute of Economy, *Trade and Industry (RIETI) Discussion Paper Series* 02-E-007, June, Tokyo: RIETI.

Nakagawa, W. and Liang, W. (2011). 'A Comparison of the FTA Strategies of Japan and China and Their Implications for Multilateralism', *Research Centre for Chinese Politics & Business Working Paper Series*, No.11, Indiana University.

Naoko, M. (2002). 'Whither East Asian Economic Integration?' *Discussion Papers (2002)*: 1–38.

Nicolas. F. (2012). 'Korea, China and economic integration in East Asia – The way forward', in *The Association of Korean Economic Studies (AKES), Korea's Role in Asian Integration*, Seoul: AKES, pp. 87–93.

Nugroho, G. (2008).'China's Preferences in the Establishment of an East Asian Free Trade Agreement: An ASEAN+3 FTA or/and an ASEAN+6 FTA?' Waseda, 19 August 2008. www.waseda-giari.jp/sysimg/imgs/200808si_19_nugroho_paper.pdf [accessed on 20 November 2017].

Office of the United States Trade Representative (USTR): https://ustr.gov/trade-agreements/free-trade-agreements/transpacific-partnership [accessed on 16 August 2017].

Padden, B. (2017). 'China Objects to THAAD, South Korea's Tourism, Imports Suffer', VOA, 30/03/2017, www.voanews.com/a/china-objects-to-thaad-south-korea-tourism/3788460.html [accessed on 14 January 2018].

Panagariya, A. (2000). 'Preferential Trade Liberalization: The Traditional Theory and New Developments', *Journal of Economic Literature*, 38(2): 287–331.

Panda, A. (2017). 'Straight from the US State Department: The 'Pivot' to Asia is Over', *The Diplomat*, 14 March 2017.

Park, S. H. and Koo, M. G. (2007). 'Forming a Cross-Regional Partnership: The South Korea-Chile FTA and Its Implications', *Pacific Affairs*, 80(2): 259–278.

Pempel, T. J. (2005a). 'Introduction: Emerging Webs of Regional Connectedness', in T. J. Pempel (ed.), *Remapping East Asia: The Construction of a Region*, Ithaca, NY: Cornell University Press, pp. 1–30.

Pempel, T. J. (ed.) (2005b). *Remapping East Asia: The Construction of a Region*, Ithaca, NY, Cornell University Press.

Porter, M. (1998). 'Clusters and the New Economics of Competition', *Harvard Business Review*, 76(6): 77–90.

Ravenhill, J. (2003). 'The New Bilateralism in the Asia Pacific', *Third World Quarterly*, 24(2): 299–371.

Reynolds, I. and Tweed, D. (2018). 'Why a Trans-Pacific Partnership without the US is Still a Big Deal', *The Edge Financial Daily*, 26 January 2018, p. 16.

Ricardo, D. (1817). *On the Principles of Political Economy and Taxation*, London: John Murray.

Riedel, J. (1991). 'Intra-Asian Trade and Investment', *Asian Development Review*, 9(1): 111–146.

Sakaki, A. and Wacker, G. (2017). '*China – Japan – South Korea; A Tense Ménage à Trois*', *SWP Research Paper*, RR 5, Berlin: SWP.

Scalapino, R. A. (1998). 'The Changing Order in Northeast Asia and the Prospects for U.S.-Japan China-Korea Relations', *UC San Diego Policy Paper 47*, California: Institute on Global Conflict and Cooperation, University of California.

Schott, J. J., Jung, E. J. and Cimino-Isaacs, C. (2015). 'An Assessment of the Korea-China Free Trade Agreement', *Policy Brief* No. PB15–24, December, Washington, DC: Peterson Institute for International Economics.

Sherwood, D and Iturrieta, F. (2018). 'Asia-Pacific Nations Sign Sweeping Trade Deal Without U.S.', Reuters, March 2018. www.reuters.com/article/us-trade-tpp/asia-pacific-nations-sign-sweeping-trade-deal-without-u-s-idUSKCN1GK0JM [accessed on 12 March 2018].

Sohn, B. H. (1995). *Linear Free Trade Area Model to Form a Northeast Asian Economic Cooperation Area*, Seoul: Korea Institute for International Economic Policy (in Korean).

Solis, M. (2017).'Trump Withdrawing from the Trans-Pacific Partnership', Brookings, 24/03/2017. www.brookings.edu/blog/unpacked/2017/03/24/trump-withdrawing-from-the-trans-pacific-partnership/ [accessed on 05 March 2018].

Solis, M. and Katada, S. (2007). 'Understanding East Asian Cross-Regionalism: An Analytical Framework', *Pacific Affairs*, 80(2): 229–257.

Spitzer, K. (2012). 'War's Legacy Plagues Japan and Its Neighbours', *Time US*, 16 August.

Stewart, E. (2018). 'Trump's Trade War Will Hurt Everyone – The Only Question is How Much', VOX, 4 March 2018, www.vox.com/policy-and-politics/2018/3/4/17078240/trump-tariffs-trade-war-steel-aluminum [accessed on 05 March 2018].

Stokes, B. and Stewart, R. (2016). "Hostile Neighbors: China vs. Japan". Pew Research Centre. (www.pewglobal.org/2016/09/13/hostile-neighbors-china-vs-japan/) [accessed on 31 August 2017].

Straits Times. (2018).'6 things to know about the trans-Pacific trade pact CPTPP', Straits Times, 23 January 2018, www.straitstimes.com/world/6-things-to-know-about-the-trans-pacific-trade-pact-cptpp [accessed on 15 February 2018].

Taiwan Bureau of Foreign Trade, Trade Statistics: (http://cus93.trade.gov.tw/ENGLISH/FSCE/) [accessed].

Tanaka, H. (2006). 'The ASEAN + 3 and East Asia Summit: A Two-Tiered Approach to Community Building', *East Asian Insights*, 1, Japan Centre for International Exchange (www.jcie.org/researchpdfs/EAI/1-1.pdf) [accessed on 22 November 2016].

Tanaka, H. (2006). 'The ASEAN+3 and East Asia Summit: A Two-Tiered Approach to Community Building', *East Asia Insights toward Community Building*, No.1, January 2006, Tokyo: Japan Centre for International Exchange.

Tiezzi, S. (2014). 'China-Japan-South Korea Hold FTA Talks Despite Political Tension', *The Diplomat*, 05 March 2014. https://thediplomat.com/2014/03/china-japan-south-korea-hold-fta-talks-despite-political-tension/ [accessed on 12 January 2018].

Trilateral Cooperation Secretariat (2017). '*CJK Together*. Trilateral Cooperation Secretariat', http://kr.tcs-asia.org/bbs/board.php?bo_table=article_ko[accessed on 26 January 2018].

Tso, C. D. (2012). 'Trans-Pacific Partnership and China-Japan-Korea FTA: Implication for Taiwan', www.stimson.org/sites/default/files/file-attachments/Trans_Pacific_Partnership_and_China_Japan_Korea_FTA.pdf [accessed on 17 November 2017].

UNCTAD. (2006). *World Investment Report 2006: FDI from Developing and Transition Economies: Implications for Development*, New York and Geneva: United Nations.

United Nations Conference on Trade and Development (UNCTAD) (2015). *UNCTAD Statistics Handbook*: http://unctad.org/en/Pages/statistics.aspx [accessed on 20 June 2016].

Vernon, R. (1966). 'International Investment and International Trade in the Product Cycle', *Quarterly Journal of Economics*, 80: 190–207.

Viner, J. (1950). *The Customs Union Issue*, New York: Carnegie Endowment for International Peace.

Wells, L. T., Jr. (1968). 'A Product Life Cycle for International Trade', *Journal of Marketing*, 5: 1–6.

Wolf, D. (2002). 'Agent-Structure Debate and Theories of European Integration: Bridging the Gap and Tunneling the Mountain', Paper prepared for the ECSA-Canada Fifth Biannual Conference Bigger and Better? The European Union, Enlargement and Reform, Toronto: ECSA, May 31st – June 1st.

World Trade Organization (WTO) (2015). '*Statistics*', World Trade Organization: www.wto.org/english/res_e/statis_e/statis_e.htm [accessed on 5 June 2016].

WTO (2012). '*International Trade Statistics 2012*', World Trade Organization: www.wto.org/english/res_e/statis_e/statis_e.htm [accessed on 5 June 2016].

WTO (2016). '*Statistics – Regional Trade Agreements: Facts and Figures*', World Trade Organization: www.wto.org/english/tratop_e/region_e/regfac_e.htm [accessed on 22 August 2017].

WTO (2017). *Rules of Origin*. World Trade Organization: www.wto.org/English/tratop_e/roi_e/roi_e.htm [accessed on 21 December 2017].

WTO (2017). '*The Doha Round*', World Trade Organization: www.wto.org/English/tratop_e/dda_e/dda_e.htm [accessed on 26 January 2018].

Wu, G. G. and Lansdowne, H. (eds.) (2008). *China Turns to Multilateralism: Foreign Policy and Regional Security*, London and New York: Routledge.

Wyatt, W. A. (1995). 'Regionalism, Globalization and World Economic Order', in L. Fawcett and A. Hurrell (eds.), *Regionalism in World Politics: Regional Organization and International Order*, Oxford: Oxford University Press.

Yap, J. (2005). 'Economic Integration and Regional Cooperation in East Asia: A Pragmatic View', *Philippine Institute for Development Studies Discussion Paper Series*, No. 2005–32, Manila: Philippine Institute for Development Studies.

Ye, M. (2017). 'South Korea's Free Trade Strategy and East Asian Regionalism: A Multistage Approach', *Asian Perspective*, 41(1): 147–174.

Yoshifumi, F. and Kuno, A. (2012). 'Toward a Consolidated Preferential Tariff Structure in East Asia: Going beyond ASEAN+1 FTAs', *ERIA Policy Brief*. No. 2012–03, 05/2012.

Yoshimatsu, H. (2008). *The Political Economy of Regionalism in East Asia: Integrative Explanation for Dynamics and Challenges*, London: Palgrave MacMillan.

Yoshimatsu, H. (2015). 'Diplomatic Objectives in Trade Politics: The Development of the China-Japan-Korea FTA', *Asia Pacific Review*, 22(1): 100–123.

Zelditch, M. (1962), 'Some Methodological Problems of Field Studies', *American Journal of Sociology*, 67(5): 566–576.

Zhang, G. L. (2016). 'China's Stance on Free Trade-Related Intellectual Property: A View in the Context of the China-Japan-Korea FTA Negotiations', *Asia Pacific Law Review*, 24(1): 36–59.

Zhang, Z. R. (2017). 'CJK FTA: Good Things Will Take Time', *New Finance*, 30 October 2017. http://hexun.com/2017-10-30/191431578.html [accessed on 14 January 2018].

Zheng, B. J. (2005). 'China's "Peaceful Rise" to Great-Power Status', *Foreign Affairs*, 84(5): 18–24.

Zheng, B. J. (2011). *China's Road to Peaceful Rise: Observations on its Cause, Basis, Connotation and Prospect*, London: Routledge.

Index

Note: Page numbers in *italics* indicate a figure and page numbers in **bold** indicate a table on the corresponding page.